The Ultimate Guide to Quantum Computing

Discover the Future of Technology and Learn Quantum Algorithms

THOMPSON CARTER

TABLE OF CONTENTS

INTRODUCTION

QUANTUM COMPUTING: A NEW ERA OF TECHNOLOGY

1. Setting the Stage: Why Quantum Computing Matters

- **Begin with a Vision of the Future**:
    - Start with an inspiring image of what quantum computing promises: transforming industries, solving problems previously deemed impossible, and unlocking new levels of scientific understanding.
    - Use real-world examples, like pharmaceutical breakthroughs, climate modeling, and finance optimization, to illustrate how quantum computing will directly impact daily life and global challenges.
- **The Current State of Computing and Its Limits**:
    - Briefly recap the evolution of classical computing, highlighting its achievements and present-day limitations.
    - Mention the exponential growth of data and the complexity of problems that classical computers struggle to solve—such as real-time climate simulations, drug interaction models, and optimization in logistics and transportation.

- **Introducing Quantum Computing as a Paradigm Shift**:
    - ○ Explain how quantum computing fundamentally differs from classical computing. Instead of bits that are strictly 0s or 1s, qubits can exist in multiple states simultaneously.
    - ○ Outline why quantum computing has emerged as a critical technology, emphasizing its potential to revolutionize fields constrained by classical computing's limitations.

2. Quantum Mechanics and the Science Behind Quantum Computing

- **Origins of Quantum Mechanics**:
    - ○ Provide a concise overview of quantum mechanics as a scientific discipline, including key milestones like Heisenberg's uncertainty principle, Schrödinger's equation, and the famous double-slit experiment.
    - ○ Explain the significance of quantum mechanics in revealing the counterintuitive nature of particles and forces at atomic and subatomic scales.
- **Foundational Concepts in Quantum Computing**:
    - ○ **Superposition**: Describe how superposition enables a qubit to exist in multiple states simultaneously,

allowing quantum computers to perform many calculations in parallel.

- o **Entanglement**: Introduce entanglement, where two qubits become linked, meaning that the state of one can instantaneously affect the state of the other, even over long distances.

- o **Quantum Interference**: Explain interference, which quantum algorithms use to amplify correct solutions and cancel out incorrect ones, enhancing computational efficiency.

- **How These Principles Lead to Computational Power**:
  - o Illustrate how these principles provide a powerful computational advantage, enabling quantum computers to solve complex problems that would take classical computers thousands of years.

3. The Current Landscape of Quantum Computing

- **Development Stages and Timeline**:
  - o Offer a brief history of quantum computing, from early theoretical concepts in the 1980s to modern advances in quantum hardware.
  - o Describe key breakthroughs, such as Shor's algorithm (which demonstrated quantum potential for factoring large numbers) and Google's quantum

supremacy experiment in 2019, which achieved a task unmanageable for classical supercomputers.

- **Key Players and Technologies**:
  - o Introduce leading companies, research institutions, and government agencies involved in quantum computing today, such as IBM, Google, Microsoft, and the U.S. Department of Energy.
  - o Describe different types of quantum computers, including superconducting qubits (used by IBM and Google), trapped ions (used by Honeywell and IonQ), and emerging photonic qubit systems.

- **Quantum Programming and Software Ecosystem**:
  - o Briefly discuss quantum programming frameworks like Qiskit (IBM), Cirq (Google), and Q# (Microsoft), which enable developers to experiment with quantum algorithms.
  - o Highlight the growth of cloud-based quantum computing platforms, which democratize access to quantum computing by allowing users to run algorithms on quantum processors remotely.

4. Real-World Applications of Quantum Computing

- **Optimization Problems**:
  - o Describe how quantum computing can tackle optimization problems more efficiently, benefiting

fields like logistics (optimizing delivery routes), finance (portfolio optimization), and supply chain management.

- **Drug Discovery and Molecular Modeling**:
  - o Explain how quantum computers can simulate molecular structures at the quantum level, accelerating drug discovery and allowing researchers to identify promising compounds faster.

- **Material Science and Chemistry**:
  - o Discuss how quantum computing can aid in discovering new materials by simulating atomic interactions with high precision. Applications include designing materials for batteries, solar cells, and superconductors.

- **Artificial Intelligence and Machine Learning**:
  - o Illustrate the potential of quantum computing to enhance machine learning by accelerating the training of AI models and handling high-dimensional datasets more efficiently.

5. Challenges and Limitations in Quantum Computing

- **Technical Barriers**:
  - o Describe current challenges in quantum computing, such as decoherence (loss of quantum state) and the

need for extremely low temperatures to maintain qubit stability in superconducting systems.

- **Error Rates and Quantum Error Correction**:
    - o Explain why error rates are a significant obstacle in building large-scale quantum computers, as quantum operations are sensitive to environmental interference.
    - o Briefly introduce quantum error correction techniques, which are essential for achieving reliable quantum computations but also require significant qubit resources.

- **Scalability Issues**:
    - o Highlight the difficulty of scaling quantum systems to include thousands or millions of qubits, which is necessary for practical, large-scale applications.
    - o Explain how physical layout, inter-qubit connectivity, and cooling requirements add to the complexity of scaling quantum systems.

- **Ethical and Societal Challenges**:
    - o Mention ethical considerations, such as the implications of quantum computing for cybersecurity (breaking traditional encryption methods) and the importance of equitable access to this transformative technology.

6. The Future of Quantum Computing

- **Predicted Advances in Quantum Hardware and Software**:
  - Outline expectations for the next decade in quantum computing, such as the development of fault-tolerant quantum computers, which can perform reliable computations despite errors.
  - Discuss the anticipated growth of hybrid quantum-classical systems, where quantum computers complement classical ones by handling specific tasks.
- **The Role of Quantum Computing in a Hybrid World**:
  - Describe how quantum computing is likely to integrate with classical systems, serving as a specialized tool for solving highly complex problems rather than replacing classical computers entirely.
  - Mention the potential for quantum cloud services to provide accessible, on-demand quantum computing resources, allowing more organizations to experiment with and benefit from quantum technology.
- **Quantum Computing's Potential Impact on Society**:
  - Offer a forward-looking view of how quantum computing could reshape industries, contribute to

scientific breakthroughs, and help solve global challenges like climate change and resource scarcity.

o Address the importance of ethical development and governance to ensure that quantum computing benefits society as a whole.

7. Why This Book? Goals and Structure

- **Purpose of the Book**:
    - o Explain that the book is designed to demystify quantum computing, providing an accessible yet comprehensive introduction to this complex field.
    - o Emphasize that the book aims to bridge the gap between technical knowledge and practical applications, helping readers understand not only the science behind quantum computing but also its real-world implications.
- **Who This Book is For**:
    - o Describe the target audience, such as students, professionals, and tech enthusiasts with an interest in emerging technologies who want to understand quantum computing without needing an advanced physics background.
    - o Mention that readers will gain insight into both the theoretical aspects and the practical applications of

quantum computing, making it a valuable resource for anyone curious about the technology's future.

- **How the Book is Structured**:
  - Provide a brief overview of each chapter, outlining the progression from foundational concepts in quantum mechanics to advanced topics like quantum algorithms, hardware, and real-world case studies.
  - Explain that each chapter builds on the previous one, guiding readers from basic concepts to more complex applications and industry use cases, ending with discussions on the future of quantum computing and its ethical implications.

Wrap up the introduction with a motivational statement about the potential of quantum computing to shape the future. Reinforce the idea that readers are embarking on a journey into one of the most exciting and transformative fields of modern science and technology. Encourage readers to keep an open mind as they dive into the book, as quantum computing challenges conventional thinking and opens up new ways of understanding the universe and solving problems that classical computers struggle to handle.

This structured approach will provide the foundation for a comprehensive introduction that explains the relevance, foundations, challenges, applications, and future of quantum computing, setting the stage for an in-depth exploration of the technology in the chapters that follow.

CHAPTER 1: INTRODUCTION TO QUANTUM COMPUTING

What is Quantum Computing, and Why is it Important?

Quantum computing is a revolutionary approach to computation that leverages principles of quantum mechanics—one of the most fundamental theories in physics—to process information in ways that are beyond the capabilities of classical computers. Unlike traditional computers, which process data in binary bits (0s and 1s), quantum computers use **qubits** (quantum bits) that can represent both 0 and 1 simultaneously, thanks to a unique property called **superposition**.

Quantum computing is important because it promises to solve certain types of problems that are practically unsolvable with classical computers. For example, tasks like breaking complex cryptographic codes, simulating molecular interactions in drug discovery, and optimizing vast logistical systems could all potentially be achieved much faster with quantum computers. The significance of quantum computing is often compared to the shift from manual computation to the first electronic computers—it's a technology that could fundamentally reshape industries, technology, and science.

How Quantum Computing Differs from Classical Computing

The difference between quantum and classical computing lies not only in how data is represented but also in how computations are performed:

1. **Data Representation**:
   - **Classical Computers**: Data is represented as bits, which can be either 0 or 1. This binary system is straightforward and reliable, making classical computers excellent for well-defined, step-by-step calculations.
   - **Quantum Computers**: Data is represented as **qubits**, which can exist in a state of 0, 1, or both at the same time, thanks to superposition. This allows quantum computers to explore multiple solutions to a problem simultaneously, vastly increasing processing potential.

2. **Quantum Superposition and Parallelism**:
   - In classical computing, each bit has one possible state at any given moment, and operations proceed sequentially.
   - Quantum computers, however, can operate on many states simultaneously due to superposition. Imagine having a massive parallel processor that can test

numerous solutions in parallel—quantum computers harness this by manipulating multiple states at once.

3. **Entanglement and Speed**:
   o Quantum computers also take advantage of **entanglement**, a property where two qubits become linked, so the state of one qubit instantly determines the state of the other, even if they are separated by large distances. This interdependence speeds up computation and enables highly efficient problem-solving processes.

In summary, while classical computers excel at tasks that require high precision and well-defined steps, quantum computers are ideal for solving complex, probabilistic problems with vast numbers of possible outcomes. This difference makes quantum computers particularly promising for specialized fields like cryptography, artificial intelligence, and computational chemistry.

Real-World Applications and Future Potential

Quantum computing is still in its early stages, but even in its current form, it is beginning to show potential in various fields:

1. **Cryptography and Cybersecurity**:
   o Quantum computers have the potential to break many classical encryption methods, which rely on the difficulty of factoring large numbers or solving

other complex mathematical problems. However, they also open the door to new forms of quantum-safe encryption.

- o **Example**: Financial institutions and governments are already researching quantum-safe encryption methods to prepare for a future where quantum computers might make current encryption vulnerable.

2. **Pharmaceuticals and Drug Discovery**:
    - o Quantum computing can model molecular and chemical interactions in unprecedented detail, which is crucial for discovering new drugs and treatments.
    - o **Example**: Quantum simulations can help pharmaceutical companies understand how molecules interact, reducing the time and cost of drug development and enabling the creation of targeted treatments.

3. **Logistics and Supply Chain Optimization**:
    - o Quantum computers are well-suited to solving optimization problems with vast solution spaces, such as routing logistics, resource allocation, and supply chain optimization.
    - o **Example**: Companies like DHL and Volkswagen are exploring quantum solutions to optimize delivery routes and reduce fuel consumption, potentially saving millions in operational costs.

4. **Artificial Intelligence and Machine Learning**:

   o Quantum computers could revolutionize machine learning by accelerating data analysis and model training processes.

   o **Example**: Quantum machine learning models are being developed to process massive datasets and create highly efficient pattern-recognition systems, promising advances in fields like natural language processing, computer vision, and predictive analytics.

A Simple Analogy to Understand Quantum Basics

To help understand how quantum computing works at a conceptual level, let's use an analogy with **coins** and **spinning tops**.

- **Classical Computing (Coin)**:

   o Imagine flipping a coin. When it lands, it shows either heads or tails, representing a classical bit with a state of 0 or 1.

   o In a classical computer, each bit is like a coin that can only be heads or tails—0 or 1—at any given time. All operations are performed by flipping these coins in a precise, step-by-step manner.

- **Quantum Computing (Spinning Top)**:

   o Now, imagine that instead of flipping a coin, you spin it on its edge. While spinning, the coin is in a state where it's neither heads nor tails but rather both at the same time. In quantum terms, this is called **superposition**.

o If you spin two coins and entangle them, their outcomes will be linked even if they're far apart. This is the principle of **entanglement**.

o With superposition and entanglement, quantum computers can keep coins "spinning" and linked in various ways, testing multiple outcomes simultaneously. This makes quantum computers incredibly powerful for specific types of problems, as they can handle multiple potential answers in parallel.

Through this analogy, we see that while classical computers are limited to sequential coin flips, quantum computers are like synchronized spinning tops, exploring countless possibilities at once. This unique approach to computation is why quantum computers have the potential to outpace classical computers in certain fields by enormous margins.

In this chapter, we introduced the core concepts of quantum computing, highlighting why it's a transformative technology and how it differs from classical computing. We explored real-world applications where quantum computing is beginning to make an impact and used a simple analogy to illustrate the concepts of superposition and entanglement.

As we move forward, we'll dive deeper into the principles of quantum mechanics that underpin quantum computing, helping to build a foundation for understanding how qubits, quantum gates, and circuits function in a quantum system. By the end of this book, you'll not only understand the science behind quantum computing but also gain insights into how it is poised to revolutionize industries in the near future.

CHAPTER 2: CLASSICAL VS. QUANTUM COMPUTERS

In this chapter, we'll explore the fundamental differences between classical and quantum computers, focusing on how each type handles data and when each approach is best suited to different types of problems. By examining how classical bits and quantum qubits differ in data representation and processing, you'll gain a better understanding of the unique capabilities of quantum computing. We'll also provide a real-world example comparing a traditional algorithm to a quantum algorithm to illustrate these concepts in action.

Key Differences Between Bits and Qubits

The basic building block of a classical computer is the **bit**, while the fundamental unit of quantum computing is the **qubit**. Here's how they differ:

1. **Bits**:
     - In classical computing, data is stored in bits, which can be in one of two states: 0 or 1.
     - Each bit represents a binary choice, and every operation in a classical computer involves manipulating these bits through a series of logical steps.

- o Bits are stable, and they do not change unless explicitly modified by the system.

2. **Qubits**:
    - o In quantum computing, data is stored in qubits, which can exist in a state of 0, 1, or both simultaneously, thanks to a property called **superposition**.
    - o Additionally, qubits can become **entangled**, meaning the state of one qubit is directly related to the state of another, no matter how far apart they are. This allows qubits to interact in ways that classical bits cannot.
    - o Qubits can be represented by various physical forms, such as ions, photons, or superconducting circuits, and they are often affected by environmental factors, making them more challenging to maintain.

How Classical and Quantum Computers Handle Data

1. **Classical Data Handling**:
    - o Classical computers process data by manipulating bits through predefined steps, known as algorithms. They execute these steps sequentially or in parallel, depending on the architecture.
    - o Classical computers perform well for tasks that can be broken down into binary decisions, such as

standard arithmetic operations, database searches, and logical processes.

○ Since bits are always either 0 or 1, classical computers process one possible solution at a time, which is efficient for well-defined, deterministic problems.

2. **Quantum Data Handling**:

○ Quantum computers handle data in qubits, which leverage **superposition** to exist in multiple states at once. When multiple qubits are entangled, they can perform complex calculations across numerous possibilities simultaneously.

○ Quantum computers apply quantum gates to qubits, modifying their state in ways that can explore many potential solutions to a problem at once.

○ Due to superposition and entanglement, quantum computers are not limited to binary states and can represent an exponential number of states relative to the number of qubits. For example, 2 qubits can represent 4 states, 3 qubits can represent 8 states, and so on.

○ Quantum computers are therefore suited to problems with large solution spaces, where many potential solutions need to be evaluated concurrently.

When to Use Classical Computing vs. Quantum Computing

Understanding when to use classical computing versus quantum computing depends on the nature of the task:

1. **Use Classical Computers When**:
   - **Precision is Required**: For tasks requiring exact, deterministic answers—such as standard calculations, web browsing, or word processing—classical computers are faster and more reliable.
   - **The Problem is Small to Medium in Complexity**: For routine tasks, classical computers are more cost-effective and efficient.
   - **Resources are Limited**: Classical computers are widely available, affordable, and stable, making them ideal for everyday computing needs.

2. **Use Quantum Computers When**:
   - **The Problem Involves Large Solution Spaces**: Quantum computers excel in handling large data sets with complex interdependencies, like molecular simulations, complex optimizations, and cryptographic computations.
   - **Efficiency is Crucial for Complex Calculations**: Problems that would take classical computers an

impractical amount of time to solve can sometimes be completed in seconds with quantum computers.

- o **Probabilistic Solutions are Acceptable**: Quantum computers are well-suited to tasks where approximate or probabilistic answers are sufficient, such as optimization and machine learning tasks.

Real-World Example: Comparing a Traditional Algorithm to a Quantum Algorithm

Let's explore how quantum computing provides an advantage in certain situations by comparing **Grover's algorithm**—a quantum algorithm—with a classical search algorithm.

Scenario: Suppose you are tasked with searching an unsorted database of one million entries to find a specific target value.

1. **Classical Approach**:
   - o A classical computer would perform a **linear search** through each entry until it finds the target.
   - o In the worst case, this search would take one million steps, and on average, it would take around 500,000 steps to find the target.
   - o Although classical algorithms exist to speed up sorted searches (e.g., binary search), they do not work on unsorted databases, requiring a full search.
2. **Quantum Approach (Grover's Algorithm)**:

- o **Grover's algorithm** is a quantum search algorithm that can find the target in approximately the square root of the total entries. In this case, that's around **1,000 steps** instead of one million.

- o Grover's algorithm leverages **superposition** to explore multiple entries simultaneously and **amplifies** the probability of the correct answer with each step, quickly honing in on the solution.

- o Although this may seem like a small improvement for one million entries, the difference becomes dramatic as the database size grows. For a database with one trillion entries, Grover's algorithm would require only about one million steps, while a classical linear search would need all trillion steps.

3. **Result**:

   - o Grover's algorithm illustrates how quantum computing can perform certain tasks exponentially faster than classical computing. In scenarios where search speed is critical (such as cryptography, pattern recognition, or large-scale data mining), quantum algorithms provide a powerful advantage.

In this chapter, we examined the foundational differences between classical and quantum computers, focusing on how each handles data and what each is best suited for. Classical computers use bits and excel at precision tasks, while quantum computers use qubits to tackle complex, probabilistic problems by leveraging superposition and entanglement.

By comparing a traditional search algorithm to Grover's quantum algorithm, we saw how quantum computing can offer significant advantages for certain types of problems, particularly those with vast solution spaces. As we progress through the book, you'll learn more about how quantum computers achieve these efficiencies, building on the concepts of superposition, entanglement, and quantum gates to unlock the full potential of this groundbreaking technology.

CHAPTER 3: QUANTUM MECHANICS ESSENTIALS

Quantum mechanics is the foundation of quantum computing. While quantum mechanics itself is mathematically complex, understanding its core principles—**superposition**, **entanglement**, and **wave-particle duality**—is essential for grasping how quantum computers work. This chapter offers an accessible overview of these concepts, using simple language and real-world analogies to help make sense of the unique behavior of particles at the quantum level.

Overview of Quantum Mechanics Without the Complex Math

Quantum mechanics is a branch of physics that studies the behavior of particles on the smallest scales—such as atoms, electrons, and photons. Unlike classical physics, which governs the world we see and experience daily, quantum mechanics describes phenomena that seem strange and counterintuitive. Here are some of the key differences:

1. **Uncertainty**:

- In quantum mechanics, the exact position and momentum of a particle cannot both be known simultaneously. This concept is encapsulated in **Heisenberg's Uncertainty Principle**, which states that the more precisely you know one property (like position), the less precisely you can know the other (like momentum).
- This is unlike classical objects, where we can measure both position and speed without any limitation.

2. **Probabilistic Nature**:
   - Quantum mechanics deals in probabilities rather than certainties. Instead of saying a particle is in a specific location, quantum mechanics provides a probability of where it could be. This probabilistic behavior is central to quantum computing because it allows qubits to be in multiple states simultaneously.

3. **Discrete Energy Levels**:
   - Particles in quantum mechanics occupy specific, discrete energy levels. For instance, an electron in an atom can only exist at certain energy levels, not in between them. This concept is called **quantization** and it's why the term "quantum" is used.

These principles form the basis of quantum mechanics and explain why particles behave differently on a quantum scale than they do on a classical scale. Quantum computing leverages these properties to perform computations that classical computers cannot.

Principles of Superposition and Entanglement

1. **Superposition**:
   - Superposition is the ability of a quantum particle to exist in multiple states at once. While a classical bit is always either 0 or 1, a **qubit** in superposition can be both 0 and 1 simultaneously, representing a combination of both states.
   - When we measure a qubit in superposition, it "collapses" into one of the possible states, but until measurement, it remains in a blended state of possibilities.

   Example: Imagine flipping a coin. While it spins, it is neither heads nor tails but rather in a state of both heads and tails. Only when it lands do we observe a specific outcome— either heads or tails. Superposition allows qubits to be in a "spinning" state, where they are both 0 and 1 until measured.

2. **Entanglement**:
   - Entanglement is a phenomenon where two or more qubits become linked, such that the state of one qubit

directly affects the state of the other, even if they are far apart. When qubits are entangled, measuring the state of one qubit will instantly determine the state of the other, no matter the physical distance.

o This interdependence enables powerful computational abilities in quantum computing, as entangled qubits work in sync to process information in ways classical systems cannot.

Example: If two entangled qubits are like two dice, rolling one die will immediately set the result of the other die, regardless of distance. In a quantum computer, this interconnectedness of qubits allows them to operate together in complex calculations.

Together, superposition and entanglement allow quantum computers to explore many solutions to a problem at once, giving them their unique computational power.

Wave-Particle Duality Explained Simply

Wave-particle duality is the concept that quantum particles, like photons and electrons, can behave both as particles (solid, defined objects) and as waves (spread out, continuous entities). This dual nature is a core concept in quantum mechanics and helps explain how particles can exist in multiple states at once.

1. **As a Particle**:

o When observed directly, a quantum particle such as an electron behaves like a particle with a defined location. For example, when a particle strikes a screen, we see a specific point of impact.

2. **As a Wave**:

o When not observed, quantum particles spread out like a wave, occupying multiple potential positions. This wave-like nature allows particles to interfere with each other, creating patterns that wouldn't occur if they were simply solid particles.

Double-Slit Experiment:

- In the famous **double-slit experiment**, particles like electrons are fired at a screen with two slits. If one slit is open, electrons behave like particles, creating a single line pattern on the screen. But when both slits are open, the electrons create an interference pattern, as if they passed through both slits simultaneously and interfered with themselves. This shows their wave-like behavior.

- However, if we place a detector at the slits to observe which path the electrons take, they revert to particle behavior, creating two distinct lines on the screen. This illustrates that quantum particles behave differently when observed, collapsing from a wave of possibilities to a single outcome.

Wave-particle duality is fundamental to quantum computing, as it highlights the concept that quantum particles (and qubits) do not have definite states until measured. This ability to exist in multiple states at once, like waves, enables quantum computers to perform many calculations simultaneously.

Real-World Analogy: Coins, Dice, and Quantum States

Using coins and dice as analogies can help make these quantum concepts clearer:

1. **Superposition (Coin in Motion)**:
   - Imagine a coin spinning in the air. While it spins, it represents both heads and tails at the same time. In classical computing, a coin is either heads or tails at any given moment, but in quantum computing, qubits are like spinning coins, representing both 0 and 1 simultaneously.
   - When you catch the coin, it "collapses" to either heads or tails—this is analogous to measuring a qubit, where it resolves into one state or the other.
2. **Entanglement (Linked Dice)**:
   - Imagine you have two special dice that are linked, so that rolling one die will immediately set the other die

to match it, regardless of distance. This is similar to quantum entanglement.

 o If two qubits are entangled, measuring one qubit will automatically set the state of the other. This is useful in quantum computing because entangled qubits can be used to perform complex operations in sync.

3. **Wave-Particle Duality (A Dice in All Possible Rolls)**:

 o Imagine a die that, when thrown, doesn't immediately land on a single number but instead exists as all possible numbers (1 through 6) simultaneously. While in the air, it represents all outcomes. Only when it hits the table does it land on a specific number.

 o This is similar to wave-particle duality, where a particle exists in multiple states as a wave until observed, at which point it "collapses" into a particular state.

These analogies illustrate how quantum mechanics allows particles—and, by extension, qubits—to exist in multiple states at once, to be interconnected across distances, and to behave as both particles and waves. These properties are at the heart of quantum computing, enabling quantum systems to handle complex, probabilistic computations that classical computers cannot.

In this chapter, we explored the essential principles of quantum mechanics that form the basis of quantum computing. We discussed the probabilistic nature of quantum particles, the principles of superposition and entanglement, and the concept of wave-particle duality. These principles help explain how qubits in a quantum computer can represent multiple states simultaneously, interact over vast distances, and behave in ways that allow for complex parallel processing.

Using analogies like spinning coins and linked dice, we aimed to simplify these ideas, illustrating how quantum properties enable quantum computers to handle data in fundamentally different ways. With this foundational understanding of quantum mechanics, we can now dive deeper into the technical aspects of qubits, quantum gates, and circuits, building toward a practical understanding of how quantum computing harnesses these unique principles to solve challenging computational problems.

CHAPTER 4: QUBITS – THE BUILDING BLOCKS

At the core of quantum computing lies the **qubit**, the quantum version of the classical bit. In this chapter, we'll explore what qubits are, how they work, and the different types of qubits in use today. We'll look at how qubits store and process information in unique ways and provide a real-world example of building a simple quantum state using qubits.

What are Qubits, and How Do They Work?

A **qubit** (short for "quantum bit") is the fundamental unit of information in a quantum computer, similar to how a bit is the basic unit in a classical computer. Unlike bits, which can only exist in a state of 0 or 1, qubits can exist in a state of 0, 1, or both simultaneously, thanks to a property called **superposition**.

1. **Superposition**:
   - A qubit in superposition can represent 0, 1, or both at the same time, allowing it to process multiple possibilities simultaneously. This unique capability enables quantum computers to explore many potential solutions at once, making them incredibly powerful for certain types of problems.

o Mathematically, a qubit in superposition can be represented as a combination of $|0\rangle$ and $|1\rangle$ states, often written as: $|\psi\rangle = \alpha|0\rangle + \beta|1\rangle |\psi\rangle = \alpha|0\rangle + \beta|1\rangle |\psi\rangle = \alpha|0\rangle + \beta|1\rangle$ where α and β are probability amplitudes that determine the likelihood of the qubit being measured as 0 or 1, and $|\alpha|^2 + |\beta|^2 = 1$.

2. **Entanglement**:

o Qubits can become **entangled**, meaning the state of one qubit is directly connected to the state of another, even across great distances. This unique feature allows qubits to be used in ways that are impossible for classical bits, as entangled qubits can coordinate their states to perform complex calculations more efficiently.

3. **Measurement and Collapse**:

o When a qubit is measured, it "collapses" from its superposition into a single state, either 0 or 1. Before measurement, the qubit exists in a probability distribution across 0 and 1, but after measurement, it takes on a definitive value.

o This probabilistic behavior is essential for quantum computing, as it allows algorithms to leverage probability and explore multiple outcomes simultaneously.

Different Types of Qubits (Superconducting, Ion-Trap, Photonic, etc.)

There are various physical implementations of qubits, each with its advantages and challenges. Here are some of the most common types:

1. **Superconducting Qubits**:
    - Superconducting qubits are among the most widely used in commercial quantum computers, with companies like IBM and Google relying on this technology.
    - These qubits are made from superconducting circuits that exhibit quantum properties at extremely low temperatures (near absolute zero).
    - **Advantages**: Fast processing speeds and compatibility with existing semiconductor fabrication methods.
    - **Challenges**: Requires extreme cooling (cryogenics) to operate, and the systems are sensitive to interference.

2. **Ion-Trap Qubits**:
    - Ion-trap qubits are created by trapping individual ions (charged atoms) in magnetic or electric fields and manipulating their quantum states with lasers.

- o Companies like IonQ and Honeywell use ion-trap technology, which provides highly stable qubits with long coherence times.
- o **Advantages**: High stability, long coherence times, and well-developed techniques for controlling ion states with lasers.
- o **Challenges**: Slower processing speeds and complex control systems due to the need for precise laser manipulation.

3. **Photonic Qubits**:
- o Photonic qubits use light particles (photons) to represent quantum information. They can be manipulated using optical devices and fiber networks, making them ideal for quantum communication.
- o Photonic qubits are often used in quantum networking and communication experiments.
- o **Advantages**: Naturally suited for transmitting information over long distances and not affected by electromagnetic interference.
- o **Challenges**: Difficult to store and maintain coherence over time, limiting use in large-scale computations.

4. **Topological Qubits**:

- o Topological qubits are based on exotic particles called anyons, which follow special rules that make them inherently resistant to errors.
- o This technology, currently under development by companies like Microsoft, holds promise for creating stable, error-resistant qubits.
- o **Advantages**: Potentially more robust against errors, making them well-suited for scalable quantum computing.
- o **Challenges**: Still in experimental stages, and creating anyons in a stable, controlled way remains challenging.

Each of these qubit types represents a different approach to building quantum computers, and research is ongoing to determine which type will be the most effective for scaling up to practical, large-scale quantum computers.

How Qubits Store and Process Information

1. **Quantum States**:
    - o Qubits store information through quantum states, with each qubit representing a blend of 0 and 1. Multiple qubits in superposition create an exponential increase in the possible states the system

can represent, allowing quantum computers to process vast amounts of information simultaneously.

o When two or more qubits are combined, they can represent up to 2^n states at once (where n is the number of qubits), a capability that classical computers cannot match.

2. **Quantum Gates**:

o Qubits are manipulated through **quantum gates**, which are the quantum equivalent of classical logic gates (like AND, OR, and NOT). These gates change the state of qubits in specific ways, allowing quantum circuits to perform computations.

o **Examples of Quantum Gates**:

▪ **X Gate** (similar to NOT): Flips the state of a qubit from 0 to 1 or vice versa.

▪ **Hadamard (H) Gate**: Places a qubit in superposition, creating an equal probability of being measured as 0 or 1.

▪ **CNOT Gate**: Entangles two qubits, allowing the state of one qubit to control the state of another.

3. **Processing Through Quantum Circuits**:

o Quantum gates are arranged into **quantum circuits**, which process qubits in specific ways to perform computations. These circuits are designed to take advantage of superposition and entanglement, making them fundamentally different from classical circuits.

○ Quantum circuits apply a series of quantum gates to manipulate the qubits and arrive at a final state, which is then measured to provide a solution.

Real-World Example: Building a Simple Quantum State with Qubits

Let's go through a simple example of building a quantum state using qubits and quantum gates. In this example, we'll use two qubits to demonstrate superposition and entanglement.

1. **Setting Up the Initial State**:
   ○ In a quantum computer, qubits are initially set to the state $|0\rangle$, which represents the binary 0.

2. **Applying a Hadamard Gate to Qubit A**:
   ○ Apply a **Hadamard gate** to the first qubit (Qubit A). This places Qubit A in superposition, so it is now in a state where it has an equal probability of being measured as 0 or 1.
   ○ Mathematically, Qubit A is now in the state: $|\psi\rangle A=12(|0\rangle+|1\rangle)|\psi\rangle\_A = \frac{1}{\sqrt{2}}(|0\rangle + |1\rangle)|\psi\rangle A=21(|0\rangle+|1\rangle)$

- o This means that if we measure Qubit A, we have a 50% chance of observing it as 0 and a 50% chance of observing it as 1.

3. **Applying a CNOT Gate to Create Entanglement**:
   - o Next, we apply a **CNOT gate** to entangle Qubit A with the second qubit, Qubit B. In this case, Qubit A serves as the control, and Qubit B will match Qubit A's state.
   - o After applying the CNOT gate, we have an **entangled state**: $|\psi\rangle = \frac{1}{2}(|00\rangle + |11\rangle)|\psi\rangle = \frac{1}{\sqrt{2}}(|00\rangle + |11\rangle)|\psi\rangle = \frac{1}{\sqrt{2}}(|00\rangle + |11\rangle)$
   - o Now, if we measure Qubit A as 0, Qubit B will also be 0. If we measure Qubit A as 1, Qubit B will also be 1. This entanglement means the two qubits are now linked, even though we only directly manipulated Qubit A.

4. **Interpreting the Quantum State**:
   - o This entangled state demonstrates one of the unique features of quantum computing: creating linked qubits that respond together. By setting up this entanglement, we've created a two-qubit system that can store information more richly and in more interdependent ways than classical bits.

This example illustrates how a simple quantum circuit with only two gates can create a complex state that classical systems can't replicate. By scaling up to larger numbers of qubits and gates, quantum computers can handle exponentially complex calculations, paving the way for powerful applications.

In this chapter, we examined the role of qubits in quantum computing, discussing their unique properties, types, and how they store and process information. Qubits use quantum mechanics to exist in superposition and entangle with each other, providing unprecedented computational power for certain types of problems. Different types of qubits—including superconducting, ion-trap, and photonic—demonstrate varied strengths and weaknesses as researchers explore scalable quantum architectures.

We also explored a practical example of building a simple quantum state using two qubits, showcasing how superposition and entanglement work together to store complex data. With this understanding of qubits as building blocks, we're ready to delve into quantum gates and circuits in the next chapter, where we'll see how qubits are manipulated to perform calculations in a quantum computer.

CHAPTER 5: SUPERPOSITION AND ENTANGLEMENT

Superposition and entanglement are two of the most essential principles in quantum computing, enabling qubits to perform complex computations in ways that classical bits cannot. In this chapter, we'll explore what superposition and entanglement are, why they're vital to quantum computing, and look at a real-world example of how these properties can be applied in cryptography.

Explanation of Superposition: Qubits in Multiple States at Once

Superposition is a fundamental property of quantum mechanics, allowing a quantum particle to exist in multiple states simultaneously. In the context of quantum computing, superposition means that a **qubit**—unlike a classical bit that is either 0 or 1—can be both 0 and 1 at the same time.

1. **Superposition in Qubits**:

    o When a qubit is placed in superposition, it doesn't exist solely in the state 0 or the state 1 but rather in a combination of both. Mathematically, a qubit's state in superposition is represented as: $|\psi\rangle = \alpha|0\rangle + \beta|1\rangle |\psi\rangle = \alpha|0\rangle + \beta|1\rangle |\psi\rangle = \alpha|0\rangle + \beta|1\rangle$ where $|0\rangle$ and $|1\rangle$ are the two basis states, and α and β are complex numbers that define the probabilities of measuring the qubit in either state. The probabilities are given by $|\alpha|^2$ for 0 and $|\beta|^2$ for 1, with the condition that $|\alpha|^2 + |\beta|^2 = 1$.

2. **Parallel Processing through Superposition**:

   o A qubit in superposition can represent multiple possible outcomes at once. When multiple qubits are in superposition, they collectively represent an exponential number of states, allowing a quantum computer to process many possibilities in parallel.

   o For example, with two qubits in superposition, a quantum computer can represent four possible states (00, 01, 10, 11) simultaneously. With three qubits, it can represent eight states, and so on. This exponential scaling is what makes quantum computing powerful for specific types of problems.

3. **Measuring Superposition**:

   o When a qubit in superposition is measured, it "collapses" to either 0 or 1 based on the probability distribution defined by α and β. This probabilistic collapse is unique to quantum systems and is fundamental to how quantum algorithms extract information from superposed qubits.

Explanation of Entanglement: Instant Communication Between Qubits

Entanglement is a phenomenon where two or more qubits become linked so that the state of one qubit directly influences the state of the other, regardless of the distance between them. When qubits are entangled, measuring the state of one qubit immediately determines the state of the other, even if they are separated by vast distances. This instant correlation between entangled qubits is often described as "spooky action at a distance."

1. **How Entanglement Works**:
    - Entanglement is created by interacting qubits in a way that links their states. For example, applying a **CNOT gate** (controlled NOT gate) to two qubits—one in superposition and the other in a defined state—can entangle them. After entanglement, the state of each qubit becomes dependent on the state of the other.
    - An entangled state of two qubits might look like this: $|\psi\rangle = \frac{1}{\sqrt{2}}(|00\rangle + |11\rangle)$ In this state, measuring the first qubit as 0 guarantees the second qubit is also 0, while measuring the first qubit as 1 guarantees the second is 1, even if they are physically separated.

2. **The Power of Entanglement in Quantum Computing**:
    - Entangled qubits can perform computations that require interdependent outcomes. Because entangled

qubits instantly mirror each other's state upon measurement, quantum computers can use them to perform calculations across multiple qubits with greater efficiency than classical systems.

o Entanglement allows quantum computers to perform faster and more complex calculations in fields like cryptography, optimization, and data analysis, where interdependent solutions are needed.

3. **Non-Locality and Quantum Correlation**:

o One remarkable aspect of entanglement is **non-locality**: the fact that entangled qubits maintain their link even when separated by large distances. This non-locality provides unique advantages in quantum communication and secure information transfer, which we'll explore further in this chapter's cryptography example.

Why These Properties are Critical to Quantum Computing

Superposition and entanglement are critical to quantum computing for several reasons:

1. **Enhanced Computational Power**:

o **Superposition** allows qubits to hold multiple values at once, enabling quantum computers to perform many calculations in parallel. This is key to solving complex problems more efficiently than classical computers, as quantum computers can explore vast solution spaces in a fraction of the time.

2. **Interdependent Processing with Entanglement**:
   o **Entanglement** allows qubits to be interdependent, enabling calculations across multiple qubits that are linked even when separated. This interconnectedness allows for faster processing and complex problem-solving that classical computers, which process bits independently, cannot replicate.

3. **Foundation for Quantum Algorithms**:
   o Many quantum algorithms, such as **Shor's algorithm** for factoring large numbers and **Grover's algorithm** for search, depend on superposition and entanglement to process information efficiently. Without these properties, quantum algorithms would lose their advantage over classical approaches.

4. **Quantum Cryptography and Secure Communication**:
   o Superposition and entanglement form the basis for **quantum cryptography**. Because of their probabilistic nature and instant communication properties, they provide the foundation for secure communication protocols that are theoretically immune to eavesdropping and hacking.

In essence, superposition and entanglement are what make quantum computers unique, enabling them to handle complex calculations and secure communications that are beyond the reach of classical systems.

Real-World Example: Using Superposition and Entanglement in Cryptography

One of the most promising applications of superposition and entanglement is in **quantum cryptography**, specifically **quantum key distribution (QKD)**. QKD is a secure method of exchanging cryptographic keys between two parties, using the principles of quantum mechanics to prevent unauthorized access.

Example: Quantum Key Distribution with the BB84 Protocol

The **BB84 protocol**, developed by Charles Bennett and Gilles Brassard in 1984, is a well-known method of QKD that relies on superposition and the probabilistic nature of qubits.

1. **Setting Up the Key Exchange**:
    o Suppose Alice wants to send a secure message to Bob. First, they need to establish a shared cryptographic key, which will allow them to encrypt and decrypt messages. Alice generates a random series of bits (0s and 1s), then sends them to Bob as qubits in superposition.
2. **Random Bases and Superposition**:

o Each qubit is sent in one of two possible bases (measurement orientations): the **rectilinear basis** ($0°$ and $90°$) or the **diagonal basis** ($45°$ and $135°$). In the rectilinear basis, qubits represent standard 0 or 1 states. In the diagonal basis, qubits are in superposition, with the 0 and 1 states representing different probabilistic outcomes.

o Because qubits in superposition can collapse unpredictably when measured, Alice and Bob choose random bases for each qubit. Bob, however, doesn't know which basis Alice used, so he randomly chooses his own bases to measure each qubit.

3. **Communicating and Discarding Mismatched Measurements**:

o After Bob has measured the qubits, he and Alice communicate (over a public, non-quantum channel) to compare their measurement bases. They discard any measurements where their chosen bases didn't match, leaving them with a smaller set of bits in which they are confident they measured consistently.

4. **Detecting Eavesdroppers**:

o If an eavesdropper (Eve) attempts to intercept the qubits, any measurement she makes will disturb the qubits' states, introducing detectable errors in the final key. When Alice and Bob compare a subset of their measurements to check for discrepancies, the presence of too many errors will alert them to Eve's interference, prompting them to discard the key.

- o If no eavesdropping is detected, Alice and Bob are left with a secure, shared key that they can use for encryption.

5. **Security of Quantum Key Distribution**:

- o The security of QKD lies in the probabilistic and interconnected nature of qubits. Superposition ensures that each measurement reveals only partial information, while entanglement or interference makes eavesdropping detectable.
- o Because QKD relies on quantum principles, it is theoretically immune to conventional hacking methods, making it a promising approach for secure communication.

Why Superposition and Entanglement Matter Here:

- **Superposition** allows Alice to send qubits that exist in a range of potential states, making the key distribution less predictable and harder to intercept.
- **Entanglement** could be used in advanced QKD protocols to create even more secure connections, with entangled qubits ensuring that any tampering affects both parties simultaneously, further securing the communication channel.

In this example, we see how superposition and entanglement allow Alice and Bob to securely share a cryptographic key, leveraging the unique properties of quantum mechanics to create secure communication channels that are resilient against eavesdropping and data breaches.

In this chapter, we explored the principles of **superposition** and **entanglement**—two critical properties that make quantum computing unique. Superposition allows qubits to exist in multiple states at once, enabling parallel processing, while entanglement links qubits in ways that classical systems cannot replicate. Together, these properties empower quantum computers to perform complex calculations and enable applications like quantum cryptography.

We examined the BB84 protocol as a real-world example, showcasing how superposition and entanglement can be used to establish secure communication channels in quantum cryptography. With these principles understood, we're ready to delve into the mechanics of **quantum gates and circuits** in the next chapter, where we'll see how qubits are manipulated to perform complex calculations in a quantum computer.

CHAPTER 6: QUANTUM GATES AND CIRCUITS

In classical computing, operations are performed using **logic gates** that manipulate bits. Similarly, in quantum computing, **quantum gates** manipulate qubits to perform computations. Quantum gates form the building blocks of **quantum circuits**, which are sequences of operations designed to achieve specific computational tasks. In this chapter, we'll introduce some of the fundamental quantum gates, explain how they work within quantum circuits, and walk through an example of building a simple quantum circuit for computation.

Introduction to Quantum Gates (X, Y, Z, H, CNOT)

Quantum gates operate differently from classical gates. While classical gates like AND, OR, and NOT perform binary operations, quantum gates operate in a way that respects the principles of **superposition** and **entanglement**. Quantum gates are represented by matrices that transform the state of qubits in ways unique to quantum systems. Here are some of the key quantum gates:

1. **X Gate (Pauli-X Gate)**:
   - The X gate is analogous to the classical NOT gate; it flips the state of a qubit. If the qubit is in state $|0\rangle$, the X gate changes it to $|1\rangle$, and vice versa.

- o Mathematically, it's represented by the matrix: $X = \begin{bmatrix} 0 & 1 \\ 1 & 0 \end{bmatrix}$

2. **Y Gate (Pauli-Y Gate)**:

   - o The Y gate rotates the qubit state around the Y-axis of the Bloch sphere, adding a phase shift.

   - o It's represented by the matrix: $Y = \begin{bmatrix} 0 & -i \\ i & 0 \end{bmatrix}$

   - o The Y gate can be used for more complex state rotations, particularly in combination with other gates.

3. **Z Gate (Pauli-Z Gate)**:

   - o The Z gate applies a phase shift, flipping the sign of the $|1\rangle$ state. It leaves $|0\rangle$ unchanged and changes $|1\rangle$ to $-|1\rangle$.

   - o Represented by: $Z = \begin{bmatrix} 1 & 0 \\ 0 & -1 \end{bmatrix}$

4. **H Gate (Hadamard Gate)**:

   - o The Hadamard (H) gate is essential for creating **superposition**. It transforms a qubit from a definite state ($|0\rangle$ or $|1\rangle$) into a superposition of both.

   - o If a qubit starts in $|0\rangle$, applying the H gate puts it into an equal superposition of $|0\rangle$ and $|1\rangle$.

- o Represented by: $H=\frac{1}{\sqrt{2}}\begin{bmatrix} 1 & 1 \\ 1 & -1 \end{bmatrix}$ H = \frac{1}{\sqrt{2}} \begin{bmatrix} 1 & 1 \\ 1 & -1 \end{bmatrix} $H=\frac{1}{\sqrt{2}}\begin{bmatrix} 1 & 1 \\ 1 & -1 \end{bmatrix}$

5. **CNOT Gate (Controlled-NOT Gate)**:
   - o The CNOT gate is a two-qubit gate and is vital for creating **entanglement**. It flips the state of the target qubit only if the control qubit is in the state $|1\rangle$.
   - o For instance, if the control qubit is $|1\rangle$ and the target qubit is $|0\rangle$, the CNOT gate will flip the target qubit to $|1\rangle$. If the control qubit is $|0\rangle$, the target qubit remains unchanged.
   - o The CNOT gate is represented by the matrix: $CNOT=\begin{bmatrix} 1 & 0 & 0 & 0 \\ 0 & 1 & 0 & 0 \\ 0 & 0 & 0 & 1 \\ 0 & 0 & 1 & 0 \end{bmatrix}$ CNOT = \begin{bmatrix} 1 & 0 & 0 & 0 \\ 0 & 1 & 0 & 0 \\ 0 & 0 & 0 & 1 \\ 0 & 0 & 1 & 0 \end{bmatrix} $CNOT=\begin{bmatrix} 1 & 0 & 0 & 0 \\ 0 & 1 & 0 & 0 \\ 0 & 0 & 0 & 1 \\ 0 & 0 & 1 & 0 \end{bmatrix}$

These gates, when combined, create quantum circuits that perform calculations by altering qubit states in complex ways.

Building Blocks of Quantum Circuits

A **quantum circuit** is a sequence of quantum gates applied to one or more qubits to perform a computation. Quantum circuits are typically represented by diagrams where qubits are shown as horizontal lines and gates are shown as symbols or boxes along those lines.

1. **Qubits as Circuit Wires**:
    - o In a quantum circuit, each qubit is represented as a horizontal line, like a wire in an electrical circuit. Gates are applied along the qubit line in the order they appear.

2. **Sequential and Parallel Operations**:
    - o Gates can be applied sequentially (one after another) or in parallel (simultaneously on different qubits) within the same circuit.
    - o The order and combination of gates determine the final state of the qubits, creating the desired computational effect.

3. **Measurement**:
    - o At the end of the circuit, qubits are measured to obtain a classical result, as qubit states "collapse" into either 0 or 1 upon measurement. This measurement is crucial because it extracts useful information from the quantum computation.

How Quantum Gates Manipulate Qubits

Quantum gates transform qubits by altering their quantum state. Here's how some of the gates manipulate qubits:

1. **Creating Superposition with the H Gate**:
    - o Applying the H gate to a qubit in the $|0\rangle$ state transforms it into a superposition of $|0\rangle$ and $|1\rangle$. This

allows the qubit to represent both states simultaneously, enabling parallel computations.

2. **Flipping Qubits with the X Gate**:
   o The X gate flips a qubit's state, changing $|0\rangle$ to $|1\rangle$ or $|1\rangle$ to $|0\rangle$. In combination with other gates, it enables more complex state manipulations.

3. **Entangling Qubits with the CNOT Gate**:
   o Applying a CNOT gate with one qubit in superposition (using the H gate) and another in a defined state ($|0\rangle$) entangles the two qubits. This entangled state creates a dependency between the qubits, allowing them to work together in a way that's essential for certain quantum computations.

By combining these gates in specific sequences, we can construct quantum circuits to solve a wide range of problems, from basic arithmetic to complex algorithms.

Real-World Example: Creating a Quantum Circuit for Simple Computation

Let's build a basic quantum circuit that demonstrates superposition and entanglement, performing a simple computation in the process.

Goal: Create a circuit with two qubits where the first qubit is put into superposition and then entangled with the second qubit. We'll measure the qubits at the end to see the resulting entangled state.

1. **Initialize the Qubits**:
   - Start with two qubits, Qubit A and Qubit B, both in the $|0\rangle$ state.

2. **Step 1: Apply the Hadamard Gate to Qubit A**:
   - Apply an H gate to Qubit A to put it into superposition. After this operation, Qubit A is in an equal superposition of $|0\rangle$ and $|1\rangle$:
   $|\psi\rangle A=12(|0\rangle+|1\rangle)|\psi\rangle\_A = \frac{1}{\sqrt{2}}(|0\rangle + |1\rangle)|\psi\rangle A=21(|0\rangle+|1\rangle)$
   - Now, Qubit A represents both states simultaneously.

3. **Step 2: Apply the CNOT Gate with Qubit A as the Control and Qubit B as the Target**:
   - Next, apply a CNOT gate where Qubit A (now in superposition) is the control qubit, and Qubit B is the target. This operation entangles the two qubits.
   - The resulting entangled state of the two qubits is:
   $|\psi\rangle=12(|00\rangle+|11\rangle)|\psi\rangle = \frac{1}{\sqrt{2}}(|00\rangle + |11\rangle)|\psi\rangle=21(|00\rangle+|11\rangle)$
   - In this state, if we measure Qubit A and get 0, Qubit B will also be 0. If we measure Qubit A and get 1, Qubit B will also be 1. The two qubits are now linked, or entangled.

4. **Step 3: Measure Both Qubits**:
   - When we measure the qubits, we'll find that they are in either the state $|00\rangle$ or the state $|11\rangle$, with equal

probability. This measurement result demonstrates the entangled state: both qubits yield the same outcome due to their interdependent states.

Interpretation:

- This simple circuit creates an entangled pair of qubits, where the outcome of one qubit directly determines the outcome of the other. It shows how quantum gates manipulate qubits to achieve superposition and entanglement, essential operations for quantum computation.

This example demonstrates the basics of building a quantum circuit, applying specific gates to create complex quantum states that can be used in computations. While this circuit is simple, the same principles can be scaled up with more qubits and more complex gate sequences to tackle advanced computational problems.

In this chapter, we introduced **quantum gates**—the fundamental tools used to manipulate qubits in a quantum computer. Gates like the X, Y, Z, H, and CNOT transform qubits in unique ways, allowing quantum circuits to perform computations through superposition and entanglement. Quantum circuits combine these gates in sequences, applying them to qubits to achieve the desired computational results.

We demonstrated a basic quantum circuit that puts one qubit in superposition and entangles it with a second qubit, illustrating how quantum gates enable complex states and interdependencies between qubits. With this foundation in quantum gates and circuits, we're now prepared to dive into **quantum algorithms** in the next chapter, exploring how specific arrangements of gates solve complex problems more efficiently than classical methods.

CHAPTER 7: QUANTUM ALGORITHMS 101

Quantum algorithms are specially designed to take advantage of the unique properties of quantum mechanics—such as **superposition** and **entanglement**—to perform computations more efficiently than classical algorithms for certain types of problems. In this chapter, we'll explore some of the most important quantum algorithms, how they differ from classical ones, when to use them, and a real-world example comparing quantum and classical search algorithms.

Overview of Key Quantum Algorithms: Shor's, Grover's, and Others

Some quantum algorithms have demonstrated remarkable efficiency for specific tasks, making them ideal candidates for problems where classical algorithms fall short. Let's look at some key quantum algorithms and what they accomplish.

1. **Shor's Algorithm**:
   o Shor's algorithm, developed by Peter Shor in 1994, is designed for **integer factorization**—breaking down a large number into its prime factors. This task is crucial in cryptography, as many encryption systems (like RSA) rely on the difficulty of factoring large numbers as a security measure.
   o **Efficiency**: Shor's algorithm can factor numbers in polynomial time, whereas classical algorithms take

exponential time for large numbers. This dramatic speedup threatens to break classical cryptographic systems if scalable quantum computers become available.

- o **Impact**: Shor's algorithm could lead to a revolution in cryptography, as it would make traditional encryption systems vulnerable to quantum attacks. This has led to the development of **quantum-safe cryptography** as a future-proofing measure.

2. **Grover's Algorithm**:

- o Grover's algorithm, developed by Lov Grover in 1996, provides a speedup for **unsorted database searches**. It allows a quantum computer to search an unsorted list of NNN items in approximately $N\sqrt{N}N$ steps, rather than NNN steps as required by a classical linear search.

- o **Efficiency**: While Grover's algorithm does not offer exponential speedup, it provides a quadratic speedup, which is significant for large datasets.

- o **Applications**: Grover's algorithm is useful for a variety of search problems, including finding matches in unsorted data, solving certain optimization problems, and accelerating brute-force password searches.

3. **Deutsch-Jozsa Algorithm**:

o The Deutsch-Jozsa algorithm was one of the first quantum algorithms to show that quantum computers could solve some problems faster than classical computers. It determines whether a given function is **constant** (same output for all inputs) or **balanced** (equal outputs of 0 and 1).

o **Efficiency**: The algorithm can solve this problem with just one evaluation of the function, while a classical algorithm might need multiple evaluations.

o **Impact**: Although more of a theoretical breakthrough than a practical one, the Deutsch-Jozsa algorithm demonstrated the potential power of quantum computing and paved the way for more practical algorithms.

4. **Quantum Fourier Transform (QFT)**:

o The Quantum Fourier Transform is a quantum equivalent of the classical Fourier transform, a mathematical operation essential in signal processing, image compression, and more.

o **Application**: QFT is a core component in many quantum algorithms, including Shor's algorithm. It enables quantum computers to solve problems related to periodicity and frequency analysis.

o **Efficiency**: QFT is exponentially faster than the classical Fourier transform, which is a significant speedup for applications in signal processing, cryptography, and pattern recognition.

These algorithms demonstrate the ability of quantum computers to solve specific problems more efficiently than classical computers, particularly in areas like cryptography, database searching, and mathematical transformations.

How Quantum Algorithms Differ from Classical Ones

Quantum algorithms differ fundamentally from classical algorithms in the following ways:

1. **Leveraging Superposition and Parallelism**:
   - Classical computers process one possible solution at a time. Quantum algorithms, by using qubits in superposition, explore multiple potential solutions simultaneously. This parallelism allows quantum computers to evaluate vast solution spaces in a fraction of the time it would take a classical computer.

2. **Quantum Interference**:
   - Quantum algorithms harness interference patterns to amplify the probability of correct answers while diminishing the probability of incorrect ones. By carefully designing quantum circuits, quantum algorithms manipulate these interference effects to zero in on optimal solutions.

3. **Entanglement**:
   o Quantum algorithms can entangle qubits, creating interdependencies between their states. Entanglement allows quantum computers to perform complex operations across multiple qubits simultaneously, something classical algorithms cannot replicate.

4. **Probabilistic Nature**:
   o Quantum algorithms often produce probabilistic results, where the solution is obtained with high probability but not certainty. Repeating the algorithm multiple times can boost confidence in the result, though this is still faster than classical approaches for certain problems.

These distinctions make quantum algorithms uniquely powerful for problems that involve large datasets, complex patterns, or probabilistic outcomes.

When to Use Quantum Algorithms

Quantum algorithms are most effective for problems that classical algorithms struggle with. Here are some scenarios where quantum algorithms excel:

1. **Cryptography**:

- o Quantum algorithms like Shor's can factor large numbers quickly, breaking the security of classical cryptographic systems based on integer factorization or discrete logarithms.
- o Quantum-safe cryptography is being developed to prepare for a future where quantum algorithms could threaten data security.

2. **Database Search and Optimization**:
   - o Grover's algorithm provides a faster way to search through large, unsorted databases, making it suitable for applications in data mining, AI, and optimization.

3. **Quantum Simulation**:
   - o Quantum algorithms are well-suited for simulating quantum systems, such as molecules in chemistry or materials in physics. Classical computers struggle with these simulations due to the vast number of variables, but quantum computers can handle them naturally.

4. **Pattern Recognition and Machine Learning**:
   - o Quantum algorithms are being explored for pattern recognition tasks in machine learning. Quantum parallelism and interference could enable faster model training and data analysis for large, complex datasets.

Quantum algorithms should be used in cases where they offer a significant speedup or efficiency gain over classical approaches. However, due to the challenges in building and scaling quantum hardware, these applications are still in the experimental stage.

Real-World Example: Quantum Search vs. Classical Search

To illustrate the power of quantum algorithms, let's compare a classical search algorithm with Grover's quantum search algorithm.

Scenario: Suppose we need to find a target item in an unsorted database with one million entries.

1. **Classical Search**:
   - A classical computer would use a linear search, checking each entry one by one until it finds the target.
   - On average, this process would take 500,000 steps (or one million in the worst case), as each entry must be examined individually.

2. **Quantum Search (Grover's Algorithm)**:
   - Grover's algorithm can search an unsorted database in about $N\sqrt{N}N$ steps, where NNN is the total number of entries. In this case, with $N=1,000,000N = 1,000,000N=1,000,000$, Grover's algorithm would only require about 1,000 steps to locate the target item.

- o This is a **quadratic speedup** over classical search, which becomes more pronounced as the database size grows. For a database of one trillion entries, Grover's algorithm would require about one million steps, while a classical search would take one trillion.

3. **Practical Implications**:
   - o This speedup is particularly valuable in fields where data is vast and unordered, such as cryptography, artificial intelligence, and optimization.
   - o While Grover's algorithm doesn't offer exponential speedup, its quadratic improvement can reduce search time significantly for large datasets, making it highly advantageous in big data applications.

4. **Quantum Circuit for Grover's Algorithm**:
   - o Grover's algorithm relies on a quantum circuit that prepares an initial superposition of all possible states, applies an **oracle** (a function that marks the target item), and then applies **Grover's diffusion operator** to amplify the probability of the marked item.
   - o By repeating this process, the algorithm gradually increases the probability of measuring the correct answer, yielding a solution with high confidence after about $N\sqrt{N}N$ iterations.

Conclusion: While classical search algorithms check each item one at a time, Grover's algorithm leverages quantum parallelism and interference to converge on the correct answer faster. This ability to speed up search tasks makes Grover's algorithm a powerful tool for applications involving large, unsorted datasets.

In this chapter, we explored some of the key quantum algorithms, including **Shor's algorithm** for factorization, **Grover's algorithm** for search, and **Deutsch-Jozsa** and **Quantum Fourier Transform** algorithms, which demonstrate the unique capabilities of quantum computers. Quantum algorithms differ from classical ones by leveraging superposition, entanglement, and interference, enabling them to solve complex problems more efficiently.

We discussed when quantum algorithms are most beneficial, particularly in fields like cryptography, database search, and quantum simulation, where classical approaches struggle. Through a comparison of Grover's algorithm with classical search, we saw how quantum search offers a quadratic speedup, demonstrating the practical advantages of quantum algorithms.

With this foundational understanding of quantum algorithms, we're now ready to dive into **quantum computers in the real world** in the next chapter, exploring how these algorithms and principles are implemented on actual quantum hardware and what challenges remain in the field.

CHAPTER 8: QUANTUM COMPUTERS IN THE REAL WORLD

Quantum computing has made significant strides in recent years, with several companies now offering real-world quantum hardware and cloud-based access to these powerful systems. In this chapter, we'll explore some of the major players in quantum computing hardware, the unique challenges of building and maintaining quantum computers, and how cloud platforms provide remote access to quantum computing. We'll also walk through a real-world example of running a basic quantum algorithm on a cloud platform.

Current Quantum Computing Hardware: IBM, Google, Rigetti, and Others

Several tech companies are leading the development of quantum computers, each utilizing different approaches and hardware architectures:

1. **IBM Quantum**:
   o IBM is a pioneer in quantum computing, offering a line of superconducting quantum computers under the IBM Quantum brand.

- o IBM's quantum processors use superconducting qubits, which operate at extremely low temperatures to achieve stability and minimize errors.
- o IBM offers cloud-based access to their quantum computers through **IBM Q Experience** and **IBM Quantum Network**, allowing researchers, students, and businesses to experiment with quantum algorithms on real hardware.

2. **Google Quantum AI**:
   - o Google's quantum computing program, Quantum AI, also relies on superconducting qubits. In 2019, Google claimed to have achieved **quantum supremacy** with their 53-qubit processor, **Sycamore**.
   - o Sycamore demonstrated a quantum computation that Google reported would take classical supercomputers thousands of years to complete.
   - o Google continues to develop its hardware and recently launched an open-source platform, **Cirq**, which allows researchers to develop and run quantum algorithms specifically for Google's hardware.

3. **Rigetti Computing**:
   - o Rigetti is a quantum computing company that builds and operates quantum processors based on superconducting qubits.

- o Rigetti's quantum computers are accessible through the cloud-based **Forest** platform, which integrates with traditional computing resources for hybrid quantum-classical applications.

- o Rigetti is known for its focus on **hybrid quantum computing**, allowing classical and quantum computers to work together on complex problems.

4. **D-Wave Systems**:

- o Unlike IBM, Google, and Rigetti, which focus on gate-based quantum computing, D-Wave specializes in **quantum annealing**.

- o Quantum annealers are particularly suited for optimization problems and are less versatile than gate-based quantum computers. However, they offer a more accessible form of quantum computing, with up to 5,000 qubits in some models.

- o D-Wave's systems are used in industries like finance, logistics, and manufacturing, where optimization is critical.

5. **Honeywell Quantum Solutions (now Quantinuum)**:

- o Honeywell uses **trapped-ion technology** for its quantum computers, a different approach that leverages ions (charged atoms) as qubits.

- o Trapped-ion qubits are highly stable and offer long coherence times, which improves error rates and makes Honeywell's systems one of the most accurate in the field.

o Honeywell has been collaborating with other tech giants and academia to advance quantum computing applications in industries such as energy, aerospace, and materials science.

Each of these companies is advancing quantum computing in unique ways, contributing to the broader ecosystem and making quantum technology accessible for experimentation and application.

Challenges with Quantum Hardware (Temperature, Stability, Error Rates)

Despite the progress in quantum computing hardware, significant technical challenges remain:

1. **Temperature Requirements**:
    o Superconducting qubits, the most common type used in IBM and Google's quantum computers, must be cooled to temperatures near absolute zero to reduce thermal noise and maintain stability.
    o Cryogenic cooling systems are expensive and complex, making it challenging to build large-scale quantum systems.

2. **Qubit Stability and Coherence**:

- o Quantum states are highly sensitive to external interference, such as electromagnetic fields, temperature fluctuations, and even cosmic rays.
- o **Coherence time** refers to the length of time a qubit can maintain its quantum state. Longer coherence times allow for more complex calculations but are difficult to achieve due to the environment's impact on qubit stability.

3. **Error Rates and Quantum Decoherence**:
   - o Quantum errors occur when qubits lose their state, due to interactions with their environment or operational faults. This phenomenon, known as **decoherence**, limits the accuracy of quantum computations.
   - o Error rates are currently high, which means that today's quantum computers need extensive error correction to perform reliable calculations. **Quantum error correction** is an active area of research but requires many additional qubits, making it costly and complex.

4. **Scalability**:
   - o Scaling up the number of qubits without losing stability is challenging. Many qubits are needed to perform error correction and maintain computational

accuracy, but adding more qubits increases complexity, error rates, and cooling requirements.

o Achieving **quantum supremacy** for practical, real-world problems remains a long-term goal, as today's quantum computers are still limited by these scalability challenges.

These obstacles are slowing the development of quantum computers capable of solving large-scale practical problems, but researchers are actively working on solutions.

Cloud Access to Quantum Computers (IBM Q, AWS Braket, Microsoft Azure Quantum)

Recognizing the challenges of building and maintaining quantum hardware, several cloud platforms now offer access to quantum computers, allowing users to run quantum algorithms remotely:

1. **IBM Q**:
   o IBM was one of the first companies to provide cloud access to quantum hardware through **IBM Q Experience**.
   o IBM Q Experience offers free and premium access to IBM's quantum computers, as well as a cloud-based development environment with the **Qiskit** open-source framework, enabling users to create and run quantum circuits on IBM's hardware.

2. **AWS Braket**:

   o Amazon Web Services (AWS) launched **AWS Braket**, a fully managed quantum computing service that provides access to quantum hardware from multiple providers, including Rigetti, D-Wave, and IonQ.

   o Braket allows users to explore different types of quantum systems and includes classical simulators for testing quantum algorithms before running them on actual hardware.

3. **Microsoft Azure Quantum**:

   o **Azure Quantum** is Microsoft's quantum computing platform, offering access to quantum hardware from companies like IonQ and Honeywell, as well as classical simulators and resource management tools.

   o Azure Quantum also integrates with **Q#**, Microsoft's quantum programming language, enabling seamless deployment and scaling of quantum algorithms on Microsoft's cloud infrastructure.

These platforms lower the barrier to entry for quantum computing, allowing researchers, developers, and businesses to experiment with quantum algorithms and understand the technology without investing in costly hardware.

Real-World Example: Running a Basic Algorithm on a Quantum Cloud Platform

Let's walk through an example of running a simple quantum algorithm—**Grover's search algorithm**—on IBM Q's cloud platform.

Objective: Use Grover's algorithm to find a target item in a small, unsorted list. This example illustrates how a quantum cloud platform works in practice.

1. **Setting Up the Environment**:
    o   Start by signing up for IBM Q Experience and accessing the Qiskit environment, IBM's open-source quantum development framework.
    o   Within Qiskit, we can write Python code to define and simulate our quantum circuits, allowing us to run algorithms either on IBM's simulators or real quantum hardware.

2. **Programming Grover's Algorithm**:
    o   Define the **oracle** function, which identifies the target item. In a simple 2-qubit example, we'll define a target state that our quantum circuit will mark using Grover's algorithm.
    o   Create a **quantum circuit** with the necessary quantum gates to put the qubits into superposition,

apply the oracle, and then amplify the target state using Grover's diffusion operator.

o   Here's a rough outline of the code using Qiskit:

python
Copy code

```python
from qiskit import QuantumCircuit, execute, Aer
from qiskit.visualization import plot_histogram

# Create a quantum circuit with 2 qubits
qc = QuantumCircuit(2)

# Apply Hadamard gate to both qubits to create superposition
qc.h(0)
qc.h(1)

# Oracle to mark the target state (e.g., '11')
qc.cz(0, 1)  # Phase flip on the target state

# Apply Hadamard and X gates (Grover diffusion)
qc.h(0)
qc.h(1)
qc.x(0)
qc.x(1)
```

```
qc.cz(0, 1)  # Invert around mean
qc.x(0)
qc.x(1)
qc.h(0)
qc.h(1)

# Measure the result
qc.measure_all()

# Run on a simulator or quantum hardware
simulator = Aer.get_backend('qasm_simulator')
result = execute(qc, simulator, shots=1024).result()
counts = result.get_counts(qc)
plot_histogram(counts)
```

3. **Executing and Analyzing Results**:
   o Run the code on IBM's cloud simulator to test the algorithm and examine the results. If successful, you should see the target state (e.g., "11") appear with higher probability than other states.
   o To run the circuit on real quantum hardware, change the backend to one of IBM's available quantum computers. Note that due to hardware noise, results may vary slightly from the simulation.

4. **Interpreting the Outcome**:

o In the histogram, observe that Grover's algorithm has amplified the probability of the target state. This is a simple example of how quantum search can provide a speed advantage over classical search, even with a small number of qubits.

Running quantum algorithms on cloud platforms like IBM Q Experience demonstrates how accessible quantum computing has become. Despite limitations in scalability and error rates, these platforms allow users to explore quantum computing's potential for real-world applications.

In this chapter, we examined the state of **quantum computing hardware** by looking at key players like IBM, Google, Rigetti, D-Wave, and Honeywell. We discussed the challenges of building quantum computers, including temperature requirements, qubit stability, and error rates. Additionally, we explored **cloud-based quantum computing** platforms like IBM Q, AWS Braket, and Microsoft Azure Quantum, which provide accessible ways to experiment with quantum algorithms.

Through a practical example of running Grover's search algorithm on IBM Q, we illustrated how quantum cloud platforms enable users to implement and test quantum algorithms, even on limited hardware. With this understanding of quantum computers in the real world, we're ready to explore **quantum programming basics** in the next chapter, where we'll dive into coding quantum circuits and understanding the tools used for quantum algorithm development.

CHAPTER 9: QUANTUM PROGRAMMING BASICS

Programming for quantum computers is a unique experience, requiring specialized languages and frameworks designed to manipulate qubits and construct quantum circuits. In this chapter, we'll explore some of the most popular **quantum programming languages**—Qiskit, Cirq, and Q#—cover how to set up a quantum programming environment, and walk through writing your first quantum program. Finally, we'll code a basic quantum circuit using Qiskit to demonstrate a real-world example of quantum programming in action.

Overview of Quantum Programming Languages: Qiskit, Cirq, and Q#

Several quantum programming languages have emerged to support quantum computing development. Here's an overview of the three most popular:

1. **Qiskit**:
    o **Developer**: IBM
    o **Description**: Qiskit is an open-source quantum computing framework developed by IBM for use with their IBM Quantum hardware. Qiskit is based

on Python, making it accessible and easy to integrate with classical Python code.

- o **Strengths**: Qiskit provides access to real quantum hardware through IBM Q Experience and offers extensive tools for creating, visualizing, and simulating quantum circuits. It's beginner-friendly, with a large library of functions, tutorials, and documentation.

- o **Primary Use**: Qiskit is ideal for those who want hands-on experience with both quantum simulations and IBM's quantum hardware.

2. **Cirq**:

- o **Developer**: Google

- o **Description**: Cirq is a Python-based quantum computing library developed by Google for programming quantum circuits specifically on Google's quantum processors, like Sycamore. It's focused on creating circuits that work well on Noisy Intermediate-Scale Quantum (NISQ) computers.

- o **Strengths**: Cirq is modular and highly flexible, allowing users to create custom gates and define unique quantum circuits tailored to Google's hardware. Cirq also integrates well with TensorFlow Quantum, enabling quantum machine learning experimentation.

- o **Primary Use**: Cirq is best suited for users interested in Google's hardware or those who want to focus on building circuits tailored for NISQ devices.

3. **Q# (Q-sharp)**:
   - o **Developer**: Microsoft
   - o **Description**: Q# is Microsoft's quantum programming language, designed as part of the **Microsoft Quantum Development Kit**. Q# is distinct from Python and is more of a standalone language that integrates well with Microsoft's cloud service, Azure Quantum.
   - o **Strengths**: Q# is specifically designed for quantum algorithms, providing native support for quantum data types and operations. It also offers a structured approach to quantum programming and integrates well with .NET languages.
   - o **Primary Use**: Q# is a good choice for developers familiar with Microsoft's ecosystem or those interested in using Azure Quantum and Microsoft's trapped-ion hardware.

Each of these languages has unique strengths, and the choice of which to use may depend on the user's preferred hardware or programming style.

Setting Up a Quantum Programming Environment

To start programming for quantum computers, we need to set up an environment where we can code and simulate quantum circuits. For this chapter, we'll focus on setting up Qiskit with Python, but similar steps apply to Cirq and Q#.

1. **Prerequisites**:
   - Ensure you have Python installed. Qiskit is compatible with Python versions 3.6 to 3.10.
   - Install a code editor or IDE like **Visual Studio Code** or **Jupyter Notebook** for writing and testing quantum code.

2. **Installing Qiskit**:
   - Open your command line or terminal and install Qiskit using pip, the Python package manager:

     bash
     pip install qiskit

   - This will install the core Qiskit package, including tools for building, simulating, and visualizing quantum circuits.

3. **Optional: Installing Jupyter Notebook**:
   - Jupyter Notebook provides an interactive environment for writing and testing quantum code. To install it, use the following command:

bash

pip install notebook

4. **Setting Up IBM Q Experience (Optional)**:
    o If you want to run your quantum code on real hardware, sign up for an IBM Q Experience account at IBM Quantum.
    o After creating an account, retrieve your API token from the IBM Q dashboard, which allows you to connect Qiskit to IBM's quantum computers.
    o Configure your account in Qiskit with:

python

from qiskit import IBMQ

IBMQ.save_account('YOUR_API_TOKEN')

Once your environment is set up, you're ready to start coding quantum circuits and exploring quantum algorithms in Qiskit.

Writing Your First Quantum Program

Now, let's write a simple quantum program to create a basic quantum circuit with Qiskit.

1. **Importing Qiskit Libraries**:
    o Start by importing the necessary libraries:

python

from qiskit import QuantumCircuit, execute, Aer

from qiskit.visualization import plot_histogram

2. **Creating a Quantum Circuit**:

   o Create a quantum circuit with two qubits and two classical bits for measurement:

   python
   qc = QuantumCircuit(2, 2)

3. **Adding Quantum Gates**:

   o Apply an **H gate** (Hadamard gate) to the first qubit to put it in superposition:

   python
   qc.h(0)

   o Next, add a **CNOT gate** with the first qubit as the control and the second qubit as the target. This entangles the two qubits:

   python
   Copy code
   qc.cx(0, 1)

4. **Measuring the Qubits**:

   o Add measurement gates to read the results from both qubits:

python

```
qc.measure([0, 1], [0, 1])
```

5. **Running the Circuit on a Simulator**:
   - Use Qiskit's **Aer** simulator to run the circuit and get the results:

   python

   Copy code

   ```
   simulator = Aer.get_backend('qasm_simulator')
   result = execute(qc, simulator, shots=1024).result()
   counts = result.get_counts(qc)
   ```

6. **Visualizing the Results**:
   - Use Qiskit's plotting tool to visualize the measurement results:

   python

   ```
   plot_histogram(counts)
   ```

This code creates a simple quantum circuit that places one qubit in superposition and then entangles it with another qubit. By measuring both qubits, we observe the probabilistic nature of quantum states.

Real-World Example: Coding a Basic Quantum Circuit in Qiskit

Now that we've covered the basics, let's use Qiskit to build a slightly more complex circuit to illustrate quantum superposition and entanglement.

Objective: Create a circuit with two qubits where the first qubit is in superposition, and then entangle the two qubits. The resulting measurements should show correlated results due to entanglement.

1. **Setting Up the Circuit**:
   - We'll start with the same steps as above to initialize the circuit and add gates:

     python
     Copy code
     ```python
     from qiskit import QuantumCircuit, execute, Aer
     from qiskit.visualization import plot_histogram

     # Create a quantum circuit with 2 qubits and 2
     classical bits
     qc = QuantumCircuit(2, 2)

     # Apply a Hadamard gate to the first qubit to create
     superposition
     qc.h(0)

     # Apply a CNOT gate to entangle the first and second
     qubits
     qc.cx(0, 1)

     # Measure both qubits
     ```

qc.measure([0, 1], [0, 1])

2. **Running and Analyzing the Circuit**:

   o Next, run the circuit on a simulator:

   ```python
   python
   simulator = Aer.get_backend('qasm_simulator')
   result = execute(qc, simulator, shots=1024).result()
   counts = result.get_counts(qc)
   plot_histogram(counts)
   ```

   o By running this circuit, we should see a histogram showing that the qubits are either in state $|00\rangle$ or $|11\rangle$, with roughly equal probability. This outcome demonstrates entanglement: measuring the first qubit as 0 ensures the second qubit is also 0, and measuring the first qubit as 1 ensures the second is 1.

3. **Interpreting the Results**:

   o The measurement results indicate that the qubits are in an entangled state, where they are dependent on each other. This simple circuit highlights quantum properties in action, showing how quantum gates and circuits can create complex states with interdependent outcomes.

In this chapter, we introduced the basics of quantum programming by exploring popular quantum programming languages—**Qiskit, Cirq, and Q#**—and setting up a Qiskit programming environment. We then wrote a simple quantum program to construct a basic quantum circuit, adding Hadamard and CNOT gates to demonstrate superposition and entanglement.

Through a real-world example, we coded a quantum circuit in Qiskit to see how quantum operations manipulate qubits and produce entangled states, showing the power of quantum programming to create complex, interdependent states. With this foundation, you're ready to dive deeper into **quantum cryptography** in the next chapter, where we'll apply these concepts to secure data transmission using quantum principles.

CHAPTER 10: QUANTUM CRYPTOGRAPHY

Quantum cryptography is one of the most promising applications of quantum mechanics, leveraging quantum principles to secure data in ways that classical cryptography cannot match. Unlike traditional encryption methods that rely on complex algorithms and computational power, quantum cryptography uses the laws of quantum mechanics, making it fundamentally secure against eavesdropping. In this chapter, we'll explore why quantum encryption is so powerful, dive into the concept of **Quantum Key Distribution (QKD)**, understand how quantum cryptography secures data transmission, and examine a real-world example of secure communication using quantum cryptography.

Quantum Encryption and Why It's So Powerful

1. **Classical Cryptography and Its Limitations**:
    - Traditional cryptographic systems rely on complex algorithms and mathematical problems, such as **integer factorization** or **elliptic curve cryptography**. These methods are secure today because they require enormous computational power to break.
    - However, with the advent of quantum computing, classical cryptographic methods could be at risk. For example, **Shor's algorithm** could break commonly

used encryption schemes like RSA, exposing sensitive data to potential attacks.

2. **Quantum Encryption's Key Advantage**:

   o Quantum cryptography offers a fundamentally different approach, leveraging the **laws of quantum mechanics** rather than computational complexity to secure data.

   o In quantum systems, information is encoded in qubits that can exist in multiple states simultaneously. The **Heisenberg Uncertainty Principle** and **quantum no-cloning theorem** prevent data from being intercepted without detection, providing built-in security.

3. **Secure Communication with Quantum Principles**:

   o Quantum cryptography relies on properties like **superposition** and **entanglement** to transmit information in a way that is inherently secure.

   o Any attempt by an eavesdropper to intercept or measure the quantum data will disturb the system, alerting both the sender and receiver to a breach.

These unique characteristics make quantum encryption particularly powerful for secure data transmission, setting it apart from traditional cryptographic systems vulnerable to quantum computing attacks.

The Concept of Quantum Key Distribution (QKD)

Quantum Key Distribution (QKD) is the primary method of achieving secure communication using quantum cryptography. QKD enables two parties to share a secret cryptographic key over a quantum channel, making it possible to detect any unauthorized interception.

1. **What is QKD?**:
    - QKD is a protocol that allows two parties (traditionally called **Alice** and **Bob**) to exchange a cryptographic key securely over a quantum channel, such as a fiber-optic cable. QKD's security relies on the principles of quantum mechanics, ensuring that any eavesdropping attempt will disturb the quantum state and alert the parties.
    - Once a secure key is established, Alice and Bob can use it to encrypt and decrypt messages using classical encryption methods like the **one-time pad** (OTP), which is unbreakable if used with a truly random key.

2. **How QKD Works: The BB84 Protocol**:
    - The **BB84 protocol** is one of the earliest and most well-known QKD protocols, developed by Charles Bennett and Gilles Brassard in 1984. Here's how it works:

1. **Preparation**: Alice randomly selects a sequence of bits (0s and 1s) and encodes them on qubits, choosing between two different bases (rectilinear or diagonal) for each bit. For example, a 0 might be represented as a horizontal photon in the rectilinear basis or a 45-degree diagonal photon in the diagonal basis.

2. **Transmission**: Alice sends each qubit to Bob over a quantum channel.

3. **Measurement**: Bob randomly chooses a basis to measure each qubit. When Bob chooses the correct basis, he accurately retrieves Alice's bit. When he chooses the wrong basis, his measurement is random, resulting in a 50% chance of error.

4. **Basis Comparison**: Alice and Bob then communicate (over a public channel) to compare the bases they used for each qubit but not the actual results. They keep only the bits where they used the same basis, discarding the rest.

5. **Error Checking and Key Extraction**: Alice and Bob publicly compare a subset of the remaining bits to check for errors. If the error

rate is low, they assume no eavesdropper was present and use the remaining bits as a shared cryptographic key.

3. **Detecting Eavesdroppers**:

   o Any attempt by an eavesdropper (**Eve**) to intercept and measure the qubits will disturb their quantum states. This disturbance introduces errors in the key, which Alice and Bob can detect during the error-checking phase.

   o If the error rate is higher than a certain threshold, they discard the key and repeat the process, ensuring that their communication remains secure.

The security of QKD relies on the fundamental properties of quantum mechanics, making it immune to computational attacks from quantum computers. This characteristic makes QKD a robust solution for secure communication in a post-quantum world.

How Quantum Cryptography Secures Data Transmission

Quantum cryptography provides security through two main mechanisms: **quantum key distribution** and **quantum-secure encryption**.

1. **Data Transmission with Quantum Key Distribution**:

o QKD is used to securely exchange cryptographic keys between two parties. Since QKD allows Alice and Bob to detect any interception attempts, they can be confident that their key remains secret.

o Once the key is securely shared, they can use it to encrypt and decrypt messages via classical encryption schemes (e.g., one-time pad or AES). This approach allows them to maintain data confidentiality and integrity during transmission.

2. **Encryption with Quantum Secure Protocols**:

o Quantum encryption can use the shared QKD-generated key in traditional protocols or directly encode the message into quantum states. Since quantum states cannot be cloned, intercepted, or measured without detection, they offer a level of security that's currently unmatched.

o Quantum encryption provides resilience against both classical and quantum computational attacks. By using the laws of quantum mechanics, these protocols provide unbreakable security that remains effective even if an adversary has access to a powerful quantum computer.

3. **Advantages of Quantum Cryptography**:

o **Eavesdropper Detection**: QKD detects any attempts to intercept the key, as eavesdropping disturbs the quantum states and introduces detectable errors.

- **Future-Proof Security**: Because quantum cryptography relies on physical principles rather than computational complexity, it remains secure even as quantum computing capabilities advance.

- **Integrity and Confidentiality**: Quantum cryptography ensures that data integrity and confidentiality are maintained, making it ideal for applications that require high levels of security.

Quantum cryptography is ideal for secure communications in industries like finance, government, and defense, where data confidentiality is paramount.

Real-World Example: Quantum Cryptography in Secure Communications

Let's explore a real-world example of using quantum cryptography for secure communication between two parties, Alice and Bob, with QKD.

Scenario: Alice and Bob want to communicate securely, knowing that sensitive information is at risk if intercepted. They decide to use QKD to establish a secure key and encrypt their communication.

1. **Setting Up the Quantum Key Distribution**:
   - Alice and Bob connect through a QKD system using the BB84 protocol over a fiber-optic link. This link allows them to transmit quantum bits securely between their locations.

2. **Key Exchange with the BB84 Protocol**:
   - Alice generates a random bit sequence (e.g., 110011...) and encodes these bits on photons, choosing a random basis (rectilinear or diagonal) for each bit.
   - She sends these photons to Bob over the quantum channel. Bob randomly chooses his basis for each bit measurement and records his results.

3. **Public Communication and Basis Comparison**:
   - Once all bits are transmitted, Alice and Bob communicate over a public channel to compare their measurement bases, keeping only the bits where their bases matched.

4. **Error Checking**:
   - Alice and Bob use a small subset of the retained bits to check for discrepancies. If the error rate is low, they assume no eavesdropper was present and proceed with the remaining bits as their shared key.

  o If an eavesdropper (Eve) had intercepted any qubits, her measurements would have introduced detectable errors, alerting Alice and Bob to a breach.

5. **Encrypted Communication**:

  o With the shared secret key established, Alice and Bob can now use it to encrypt and decrypt messages securely. For instance, they can apply the **one-time pad** technique, where each bit of the key is combined with the message bit-by-bit, creating an unbreakable encryption.

6. **Benefits of Quantum-Secured Communication**:

  o Alice and Bob are assured of their communication's security. Even if Eve has access to a quantum computer, she cannot decrypt the messages because she was unable to obtain the shared key.

  o This setup can be extended to highly secure environments like government communications, financial transactions, and military operations where data integrity and confidentiality are paramount.

Case Studies:

- **SwissQuantum Network**: Switzerland implemented a QKD-based quantum network in 2009 to secure data between government offices and financial institutions.

- **China's Quantum Communication Network**: China has established the world's longest quantum communication network, spanning over 2,000 kilometers and linking several cities to provide secure government and military communication.

These real-world implementations demonstrate the viability of QKD and quantum cryptography in securing sensitive communication channels, ensuring that critical information remains safe even in the age of quantum computing.

In this chapter, we explored the fundamentals of **quantum cryptography**, covering why it's powerful, how **Quantum Key Distribution (QKD)** works, and how quantum cryptography secures data transmission. Unlike classical encryption, which is vulnerable to future quantum attacks, quantum cryptography provides a level of security based on the principles of quantum mechanics, making it virtually unbreakable.

We also discussed a real-world example of using quantum cryptography to establish a secure communication channel between Alice and Bob, illustrating how QKD enables safe key exchange and eavesdropper detection. With quantum cryptography already implemented in government and financial systems worldwide, it's clear that this technology has significant implications for secure communication in a post-quantum world.

Next, we'll dive into **quantum computing's role in artificial intelligence** and explore how quantum algorithms can accelerate machine learning, data analysis, and pattern recognition tasks.

CHAPTER 11: QUANTUM COMPUTING AND ARTIFICIAL INTELLIGENCE

Quantum computing holds significant promise for advancing **artificial intelligence (AI)** and **machine learning (ML)**, fields that rely heavily on complex computations and large datasets. By leveraging the power of quantum mechanics, quantum computers could accelerate data processing, pattern recognition, and optimization in AI, leading to faster and more powerful machine learning models. In this chapter, we'll explore how quantum computing impacts AI, cover the basics of **quantum machine learning (QML)** algorithms and their use cases, discuss the potential for quantum-accelerated AI, and examine a real-world example of using quantum algorithms for pattern recognition.

How Quantum Computing Can Impact AI and Machine Learning
Quantum computing has the potential to transform AI and machine learning in several ways:

1. **Faster Data Processing**:
    o Quantum computers can process multiple states simultaneously through **superposition**, enabling them to evaluate vast solution spaces in parallel. This capability could speed up data-intensive ML tasks,

such as processing large datasets and calculating complex model parameters.

- o AI applications that require significant computational power, such as deep learning and natural language processing, could benefit from quantum-accelerated data processing.

2. **Enhanced Optimization**:
   - o Many AI algorithms, particularly in ML, involve solving optimization problems (finding the best set of parameters for a given model). Quantum computing's **quantum annealing** and optimization algorithms (like Grover's) are well-suited for these tasks, as they can explore multiple configurations in parallel and converge on optimal solutions faster than classical methods.

3. **Improved Pattern Recognition and Feature Extraction**:
   - o Quantum computers can potentially recognize patterns more efficiently by analyzing large datasets in parallel, making them ideal for image recognition, medical diagnostics, and anomaly detection.
   - o Quantum-enhanced feature extraction could also improve the accuracy of AI models by identifying relevant data features faster and more accurately.

4. **Efficient Model Training and Parameter Tuning**:

○ Model training is often the most computationally demanding part of ML, requiring substantial time and resources. Quantum computing could reduce training time by accelerating matrix calculations, gradient descent, and other parameter optimization techniques, leading to faster and more efficient training of machine learning models.

These advantages suggest that quantum computing could enable a new generation of AI applications, making machine learning models faster, more accurate, and capable of handling larger datasets.

Quantum Machine Learning Basics: QML Algorithms and Use Cases

Quantum Machine Learning (QML) combines principles of quantum computing and machine learning to create algorithms that utilize quantum states and operations. Here are some basic QML algorithms and use cases:

1. **Quantum Support Vector Machines (QSVMs)**:
   ○ **Support Vector Machines (SVMs)** are a widely used classical ML algorithm for classification tasks. QML adapts this algorithm into QSVMs, which leverage quantum computing's ability to analyze large-dimensional feature spaces efficiently.

o QSVMs use **quantum kernels** to project data into higher-dimensional spaces, making it easier to separate complex data clusters.

o **Use Cases**: Image recognition, fraud detection, and natural language processing.

2. **Quantum Principal Component Analysis (QPCA)**:

o **Principal Component Analysis (PCA) is** a classical ML technique used for dimensionality reduction, helping reduce the number of variables in large datasets while retaining essential information.

o Quantum PCA uses quantum algorithms to calculate principal components more efficiently, making it suitable for large datasets.

o **Use Cases**: Data compression, noise reduction, and feature extraction in large datasets, such as genomic data analysis or financial modeling.

3. **Quantum Neural Networks (QNNs)**:

o Quantum Neural Networks aim to mimic the structure and learning process of classical neural networks while leveraging quantum computation for faster and potentially more powerful model training.

o QNNs are built from quantum circuits, with qubits representing neurons and quantum gates representing weights. QNNs can perform certain operations, such as matrix multiplications and data transformations, much faster than classical networks.

- o **Use Cases**: Image recognition, text generation, and other complex AI tasks, with the potential to train larger and more accurate neural networks.

4. **Quantum Boltzmann Machines (QBMs)**:
- o Inspired by Boltzmann machines, Quantum Boltzmann Machines (QBMs) are generative models that can learn probability distributions, making them suitable for unsupervised learning.
- o QBMs use quantum states to represent probability distributions, which can enhance the performance of probabilistic models, particularly in pattern recognition and generative tasks.
- o **Use Cases**: Image generation, anomaly detection, and natural language processing.

5. **Quantum Annealing for Optimization**:
- o Quantum annealers, such as those developed by D-Wave, specialize in solving complex optimization problems, which are prevalent in AI for tuning model parameters and hyperparameters.
- o **Use Cases**: Optimizing complex models, supply chain logistics, financial portfolio optimization, and other applications requiring fast optimization.

These QML algorithms demonstrate the potential for quantum computing to improve efficiency and scalability in machine learning, opening doors to new applications and more advanced AI models.

Potential for Faster, More Powerful AI with Quantum Computing
Quantum computing's unique capabilities—such as parallelism, entanglement, and superposition—enable AI algorithms to be more efficient, accurate, and scalable. Here's how quantum computing can drive the development of faster and more powerful AI:

1. **Accelerated Training for Large Models**:
   - Quantum computers can execute matrix operations faster than classical computers, potentially reducing the time required to train large models, such as deep neural networks and reinforcement learning agents.
   - This acceleration could lead to breakthroughs in natural language processing, computer vision, and other areas that rely on large, complex models.

2. **Scalability for Big Data**:
   - Quantum computing is inherently capable of handling high-dimensional data. By processing data in parallel, quantum computers could enable AI systems to manage vast datasets without compromising speed or accuracy.

    o Industries like finance, healthcare, and cybersecurity, where data volume and complexity are high, could benefit significantly from quantum-enhanced AI.

3. **Enhanced Decision-Making Capabilities**:

    o Quantum algorithms, like Grover's search and quantum Monte Carlo simulations, can improve decision-making by providing faster and more accurate predictions. In fields like autonomous driving, supply chain management, and robotics, quantum AI could enable faster real-time decision-making.

4. **Unlocking New AI Capabilities**:

    o Quantum computers can model complex quantum systems, enabling breakthroughs in material science, drug discovery, and fundamental physics. These discoveries can fuel AI research, making it possible to simulate and predict natural phenomena with greater accuracy.

As quantum computing continues to mature, its integration with AI could unlock unprecedented possibilities, transforming industries and redefining the potential of intelligent systems.

Real-World Example: Applying Quantum Algorithms to Pattern Recognition

One area where quantum computing shows promise is in **pattern recognition**, a foundational task in AI. Let's look at a real-world example of how quantum algorithms can improve pattern recognition, particularly in **image classification**.

Scenario: Suppose we are tasked with building an image classification system to identify whether an image contains a particular object, such as a cat. With a large dataset, classical methods may struggle with processing speed, especially as the dataset grows.

Using a Quantum Support Vector Machine (QSVM):

1. **Quantum Kernel Trick**:
   - In classical SVMs, the **kernel trick** is used to map data into higher-dimensional spaces to make classification easier. A QSVM extends this by using a **quantum kernel** to project data into a quantum state space, enabling a much higher-dimensional mapping.
   - By encoding images as quantum states, QSVMs can process high-dimensional data efficiently, reducing the computational load and improving classification accuracy.

2. **Data Encoding**:

- o Each pixel or feature of the image is encoded into a quantum state, creating a multi-dimensional feature space. Quantum circuits then manipulate these states to emphasize distinguishing features, such as edges, colors, or textures.

3. **Training and Classification**:

- o The QSVM algorithm iterates through labeled training images, calculating the optimal decision boundary between classes (e.g., images with cats vs. images without cats).

- o By leveraging quantum superposition and entanglement, the QSVM efficiently searches for this boundary, allowing the model to classify images accurately in a fraction of the time required by classical SVMs.

4. **Performance Analysis**:

- o Preliminary research has shown that QSVMs can classify images with fewer resources and at higher speeds than classical SVMs, particularly as dataset complexity increases.

- o In practical applications, this speed advantage could reduce the time required to train and deploy image recognition systems, making quantum computing a powerful tool for industries like healthcare (for medical imaging), finance (for fraud detection), and security (for facial recognition).

In this chapter, we explored the intersection of **quantum computing** and **artificial intelligence**, examining how quantum computing can enhance AI's capabilities in data processing, optimization, pattern recognition, and model training. We introduced the basics of **Quantum Machine Learning (QML)**, covering algorithms like Quantum Support Vector Machines, Quantum Principal Component Analysis, and Quantum Neural Networks, along with their specific use cases in AI.

We also discussed the potential of quantum computing to drive faster, more powerful AI by enabling efficient model training, handling large datasets, and improving decision-making in real time. Through a real-world example of using a Quantum Support Vector Machine for image classification, we saw how quantum algorithms can significantly accelerate and improve pattern recognition, demonstrating the transformative potential of quantum-enhanced AI.

In the next chapter, we'll shift focus to **quantum simulation and chemistry**, exploring how quantum computing can simulate molecules and reactions, with applications in drug discovery and material science.

CHAPTER 12: QUANTUM SIMULATION AND CHEMISTRY

One of the most promising applications of **quantum computing** lies in **quantum simulation**—particularly in the field of **chemistry**. Quantum computers have the potential to simulate molecules, chemical reactions, and quantum systems at a level of accuracy and efficiency that classical computers struggle to achieve. This ability could revolutionize industries such as **drug discovery** and **materials science** by enabling scientists to design new drugs, materials, and chemical compounds more efficiently. In this chapter, we'll explore the role of quantum computing in chemistry, examine its applications, and walk through a real-world example of using a quantum computer to simulate a small molecule.

The Role of Quantum Computing in Simulating Molecules and Reactions

Simulating molecules and chemical reactions is inherently complex. At the quantum level, particles such as electrons interact in ways that are highly probabilistic and governed by the principles of quantum mechanics. These interactions are challenging for classical computers to model accurately due to the **exponential scaling** of complexity as the number of particles in a system increases.

1. **Quantum vs. Classical Simulation**:

- o Classical computers represent molecular systems by approximating electron positions and interactions, often simplifying them to make the calculations feasible. For example, many chemical simulations rely on **Density Functional Theory (DFT)**, which uses mathematical approximations that can sometimes limit accuracy.

- o Quantum computers, on the other hand, can naturally simulate quantum systems because they use **qubits** and **quantum gates** to represent and manipulate quantum states directly. This property enables quantum computers to perform **exact quantum simulations** without the need for complex approximations, allowing scientists to achieve more accurate results for specific molecular interactions.

2. **Quantum Simulation Algorithms**:

- o Quantum algorithms like the **Variational Quantum Eigensolver (VQE)** and **Quantum Phase Estimation (QPE)** are specifically designed for simulating molecular energy states. These algorithms allow quantum computers to calculate properties like molecular ground state energies, reaction pathways, and electron distributions.

- o By calculating these properties accurately, quantum simulation provides insights into how molecules behave, interact, and react, leading to potential breakthroughs in fields where understanding molecular interactions is crucial.

3. **Scalability and Accuracy**:
   - While today's quantum computers are still limited in qubit count and coherence, researchers can simulate small molecules accurately on these devices. As quantum hardware improves, larger and more complex molecules, such as proteins and macromolecules, will become feasible for quantum simulation, opening new possibilities for chemistry and material science.

Quantum simulation holds the promise of revolutionizing fields that depend on understanding molecular structures and interactions by providing detailed, accurate simulations that could lead to new discoveries.

Applications in Drug Discovery and Materials Science

Quantum simulation has transformative potential in several key areas:

1. **Drug Discovery**:
   - Developing new drugs requires an understanding of how potential drug compounds interact with target molecules in the body. Currently, drug discovery

relies heavily on trial and error, high-throughput screening, and classical molecular modeling, which can be time-consuming and costly.

o Quantum computers could simulate interactions between drug compounds and biological targets, such as proteins, with unprecedented accuracy, enabling scientists to predict a drug's efficacy, toxicity, and binding properties early in the development process.

o This capability could shorten drug discovery timelines, reduce development costs, and even lead to the discovery of new classes of drugs for diseases like cancer, Alzheimer's, and autoimmune disorders.

2. **Materials Science**:

o Designing new materials with desirable properties, such as superconductivity, thermal stability, or specific mechanical characteristics, requires a deep understanding of the atomic and electronic structures of materials.

o Quantum simulation can provide insights into how materials behave under various conditions and predict their properties before they are synthesized in the lab. For example, quantum computers could simulate materials with high thermal resistance, lightweight strength, or superconductive properties.

    o This could lead to breakthroughs in areas like renewable energy (e.g., more efficient solar cells), electronics (e.g., more effective semiconductors), and aerospace engineering (e.g., lightweight, durable materials for aircraft).

3. **Catalysis and Chemical Engineering**:

    o Catalysts speed up chemical reactions and are essential for industries like energy production and chemical manufacturing. However, designing effective catalysts is challenging due to the complexity of reaction mechanisms.

    o Quantum simulation could help scientists design new catalysts that increase reaction efficiency, reduce energy consumption, and lower production costs. For instance, researchers could use quantum computers to simulate catalyst performance in processes like carbon capture or hydrogen production, contributing to greener, more sustainable industrial practices.

The applications of quantum simulation in chemistry could have far-reaching impacts across multiple industries, from healthcare to energy to manufacturing, by enabling more accurate predictions and optimizations for molecular and material interactions.

Real-World Example: Simulating a Small Molecule with a Quantum Computer

Let's explore a practical example of how a quantum computer can simulate a small molecule, specifically **molecular hydrogen (H_2)**. Although H_2 is a simple molecule, it's frequently used as a test case for quantum simulation due to its relatively straightforward structure.

1. **The Objective**:
   - The goal is to calculate the **ground state energy** of the hydrogen molecule, which is the lowest possible energy state of the system. Knowing the ground state energy provides insights into the molecule's stability and chemical properties.

2. **Using the Variational Quantum Eigensolver (VQE)**:
   - For this simulation, we'll use the **Variational Quantum Eigensolver (VQE)** algorithm, which is well-suited for near-term quantum devices. VQE is a **hybrid algorithm** that combines quantum and classical computation to approximate ground state energies.
   - The VQE algorithm uses a **parameterized quantum circuit** to prepare a trial wave function for the molecule and iteratively optimizes these parameters on a classical computer to minimize the energy.

3. **Steps of the Simulation**:

- **Step 1: Define the Molecular Hamiltonian**:
    - The Hamiltonian represents the total energy of the molecule as a function of its electronic and nuclear interactions. For H_2, the Hamiltonian can be calculated based on molecular properties, such as bond length.
    - Using classical pre-computation, the Hamiltonian is converted into a form that the quantum computer can understand, with each part corresponding to quantum gates in the circuit.
- **Step 2: Create a Quantum Circuit for the VQE**:
    - We set up a quantum circuit with a few qubits (typically 2–4 qubits for H_2), representing the electronic states of the hydrogen atoms.
    - Quantum gates are then applied in a specific sequence to encode the molecule's wave function. These gates are parameterized, meaning they have variable angles that the algorithm will adjust to find the lowest energy.
- **Step 3: Run the Circuit and Measure the Energy**:
    - The circuit is executed on the quantum hardware or a quantum simulator, and the resulting measurements are used to calculate

the molecule's energy for the current parameters.

- The VQE algorithm then adjusts the gate parameters using a classical optimizer, seeking to minimize the calculated energy.

- **Step 4: Iterate Until Convergence**:
  - The algorithm repeats the quantum computation and classical optimization steps until it converges on a minimum energy. This minimum energy approximates the ground state energy of the H_2 molecule.

4. **Results**:
   - For a molecule as simple as H_2, the VQE algorithm on a quantum computer or a simulator can typically yield an accurate estimate of the ground state energy.
   - This experiment shows that even with today's limited quantum hardware, quantum computers can provide insights into molecular properties without requiring the vast computational resources that classical computers need.

5. **Future Implications**:
   - While simulating H_2 is straightforward, the same principles apply to more complex molecules. As quantum hardware improves, researchers expect to simulate larger, more complex molecules accurately,

opening up possibilities for simulating proteins, enzymes, and synthetic materials that are currently infeasible to model with classical computers.

This example highlights how quantum computing can revolutionize molecular simulation, paving the way for breakthroughs in chemistry, pharmacology, and materials science.

In this chapter, we explored the significant role that **quantum computing** can play in **chemistry**, particularly in simulating molecules and chemical reactions. We discussed how quantum computers can outperform classical computers in modeling molecular systems, thanks to their ability to represent quantum states directly. This ability makes quantum simulation valuable for applications in **drug discovery**, **materials science**, and **chemical engineering**, where accurate molecular predictions are critical.

Through a real-world example of simulating molecular hydrogen (H_2) with a quantum computer, we saw how quantum algorithms, such as the **Variational Quantum Eigensolver (VQE)**, can calculate ground state energies and provide insights into molecular properties. As quantum hardware advances, we can expect to see larger molecules and more complex reactions simulated with greater accuracy, leading to discoveries in healthcare, energy, and manufacturing.

In the next chapter, we'll turn our attention to **quantum error correction**—an essential component for improving the stability and reliability of quantum computations, and a key challenge on the path to scalable, practical quantum computing.

CHAPTER 13: QUANTUM ERROR CORRECTION

Quantum error correction is one of the most critical areas of research in **quantum computing**. Due to the fragile nature of quantum states, errors are common in quantum computers, affecting calculations and limiting the scalability of quantum systems. Quantum error correction techniques aim to mitigate these issues, enabling quantum computers to perform stable and accurate computations. In this chapter, we'll examine why errors are prevalent in quantum systems, explore key error correction methods, discuss how error rates impact quantum computing power, and use a real-world analogy to explain the importance of quantum error correction.

Why Errors Are Common in Quantum Computers

Unlike classical bits, which are either 0 or 1, **qubits** exist in complex quantum states that are highly sensitive to their environment. This sensitivity makes quantum computers prone to errors due to several factors:

1. **Decoherence**:
    - **Decoherence** occurs when a qubit loses its quantum state due to interactions with its surroundings,

causing it to collapse into a definite state (either 0 or 1) prematurely.

- o Decoherence is one of the most common error sources in quantum computing and results from factors like temperature fluctuations, electromagnetic interference, and even cosmic rays.

2. **Gate Errors**:

- o Quantum gates are used to manipulate qubits in specific ways, but these gates are not perfectly accurate. **Gate errors** occur when a gate operation introduces an unintended alteration to the qubit's state.

- o The precision of quantum gate operations is crucial because even a slight deviation can affect the overall computation. Gate errors accumulate quickly in larger circuits, impacting the outcome.

3. **Measurement Errors**:

- o When a quantum operation is complete, the final state of the qubits is measured to obtain a classical result. **Measurement errors** can occur if the measurement process itself interferes with the qubit's state, leading to inaccurate results.

- o These errors are especially problematic because they affect the final readout, potentially corrupting the output of the entire computation.

4. **Noise and External Interference**:

   o Qubits are affected by external noise from the environment, which can alter their states unpredictably. This noise includes electromagnetic interference, temperature changes, and other environmental factors.

Because of these factors, errors in quantum computing are frequent, even with state-of-the-art quantum hardware. Addressing these errors through quantum error correction is essential to enable reliable and scalable quantum computation.

Quantum Error Correction Techniques (Logical Qubits, Error-Correcting Codes)

Quantum error correction techniques aim to counteract the effects of errors by encoding information in a way that allows the system to detect and correct errors without measuring the actual state of the qubit. Here are some of the primary methods used:

1. **Logical Qubits**:

   o **Logical qubits** are a fundamental concept in quantum error correction. Unlike physical qubits, which are the actual qubits in a quantum computer, logical qubits are virtual qubits encoded using multiple physical qubits.

o By encoding one logical qubit across several physical qubits, we create redundancy that can detect and correct errors. Logical qubits are designed to be resilient to small disturbances, helping the system correct errors in individual physical qubits without affecting the overall computation.

2. **Quantum Error-Correcting Codes**:

   o Quantum error-correcting codes are techniques for encoding quantum information across multiple qubits to detect and correct errors. Some common codes include:

   - **Shor Code**: Named after Peter Shor, the Shor Code uses 9 physical qubits to encode a single logical qubit. It protects against both bit-flip and phase-flip errors, making it one of the earliest and most widely known quantum error-correcting codes.

   - **Steane Code**: The Steane Code, a 7-qubit code, is designed to correct single-qubit errors and is often used in conjunction with other error correction strategies.

   - **Surface Code**: The Surface Code is a 2D lattice of qubits and is one of the most promising error-correcting codes for large-scale quantum computing. It uses neighboring qubits to detect errors, making it scalable and efficient in terms of qubit usage.

o These codes add redundancy by encoding logical qubits across several physical qubits, allowing the system to detect errors without directly measuring the state of individual qubits (which would collapse the quantum state).

3. **Syndrome Measurement**:

o **Syndrome measurement** is a technique used in error correction where additional qubits (known as **ancilla qubits**) are introduced to detect errors. Ancilla qubits interact with the logical qubits to identify the error type without collapsing the quantum state.

o Syndrome measurements reveal only the error type and location, not the actual state, preserving the overall quantum information while enabling error correction.

4. **Fault-Tolerant Quantum Computing**:

o Fault-tolerant quantum computing refers to designing quantum circuits that can continue to function accurately even when errors occur. This approach uses error-correcting codes and logical qubits to ensure that errors are detected and corrected without disrupting the computation.

- o Fault-tolerant architectures are essential for scaling quantum computers, as they help ensure that a large quantum system remains operational even with a significant number of qubits experiencing errors.

These error correction techniques are crucial for advancing quantum computing, as they enable quantum systems to perform reliable calculations despite inherent instability and error-proneness.

The Impact of Error Rates on Quantum Computing Power

Error rates in quantum computing significantly impact the power and scalability of quantum systems:

1. **Increased Computational Cost**:
   - o As error rates increase, the need for error correction also rises, which requires more physical qubits and greater computational resources. For each logical qubit, several physical qubits are needed, often in the range of dozens to hundreds, depending on the target error rate.
   - o This overhead means that more complex calculations require vastly more qubits to achieve reliable results, limiting the effective computational power of today's quantum computers.

2. **Limits on Circuit Depth**:

o Quantum circuits with multiple gate operations (referred to as **circuit depth**) are more susceptible to accumulating errors. The higher the error rate, the fewer gates that can be used in a circuit without rendering the results unreliable.

o As a result, quantum algorithms that require many gates or complex circuit structures may be infeasible until error rates are significantly reduced.

3. **Quantum Error Threshold**:

o There is a theoretical **error threshold** in quantum computing, below which quantum error correction techniques can maintain the fidelity of a quantum system. Once error rates fall below this threshold, fault-tolerant quantum computing becomes viable, enabling scalable, reliable quantum systems.

o Achieving this threshold is a major goal in quantum hardware research, as it represents a critical step toward practical quantum computing on a large scale.

Without effective error correction, quantum computers cannot perform complex calculations accurately, and their usefulness remains limited. By developing techniques to reduce error rates, researchers are paving the way for more robust and scalable quantum computing.

Real-World Analogy: Comparing Quantum Error Correction to Redundancy in Classical Computing

To understand the role of quantum error correction, we can draw an analogy to redundancy in classical computing systems:

1. **Error Correction Codes in Classical Computing**:
   - In classical computing, **error correction codes** are used to detect and correct errors in data transmission and storage. For instance, in RAID (Redundant Array of Independent Disks) systems, data is distributed across multiple disks with redundant copies, allowing recovery if one disk fails.
   - Similarly, in networking, techniques like **Hamming codes** and **parity bits** add redundant information to transmitted data, enabling the receiver to detect and correct bit errors caused by noise or interference.

2. **Logical Qubits as Redundant Data**:
   - In quantum computing, **logical qubits** function similarly to redundancy in classical error correction. By encoding a logical qubit across multiple physical qubits, quantum error correction creates redundant representations of quantum information, enabling the system to detect and correct errors.
   - Just as RAID systems protect data from disk failures, logical qubits protect quantum information from

errors in individual physical qubits, allowing the system to maintain overall fidelity.

3. **Syndrome Measurement as Error Detection**:

   o In classical computing, error detection codes are used to identify where errors occur, allowing for corrective action. In quantum computing, **syndrome measurements** fulfill a similar role, detecting errors without collapsing the quantum state.

   o By detecting errors indirectly, quantum computers can correct these errors while preserving the quantum information's integrity, much like how classical error detection methods enable corrections without requiring retransmission.

4. **Fault Tolerance as a Reliable System**:

   o Fault tolerance in quantum computing is akin to redundancy in high-availability systems, such as backup servers or data centers. These systems are designed to function accurately even when certain components fail.

   o Similarly, fault-tolerant quantum computing ensures that computations can proceed accurately, even when individual qubits experience errors, providing the robustness needed for reliable quantum computation.

This analogy helps illustrate the importance of error correction in quantum computing. Just as redundancy allows classical systems to function reliably despite errors, quantum error correction techniques allow quantum systems to perform stable and accurate calculations.

In this chapter, we delved into **quantum error correction**, examining why errors are common in quantum computers and how error correction techniques help address these challenges. We explored key methods, including **logical qubits** and **quantum error-correcting codes** like the Shor Code, Steane Code, and Surface Code, all of which enable quantum systems to detect and correct errors without collapsing the quantum state.

We also discussed the impact of error rates on quantum computing power, highlighting the importance of reducing errors to enable complex computations and achieve scalable, fault-tolerant quantum systems. Finally, we used a real-world analogy to relate quantum error correction to redundancy in classical computing, underscoring the role of error correction in building reliable, resilient quantum systems.

In the next chapter, we'll explore **quantum programming languages** and tools that incorporate error correction, and we'll discuss how they are used to implement quantum circuits that can operate reliably on today's quantum hardware.

CHAPTER 14: QUANTUM SUPREMACY AND BEYOND

Quantum supremacy is the point at which a quantum computer can perform a specific computation faster than the most powerful classical supercomputers. Achieving quantum supremacy represents a significant milestone, indicating that quantum computers can solve problems that classical computers cannot. In this chapter, we'll explore what quantum supremacy is, why it's important, examine Google's quantum supremacy experiment and its implications, discuss the ongoing race for practical, universal quantum computing, and consider the potential impacts of quantum supremacy on various industries.

What is Quantum Supremacy, and Why Does It Matter?

Quantum supremacy is the term used to describe the moment when a quantum computer outperforms classical supercomputers at a specific task. While achieving quantum supremacy does not mean quantum computers are immediately practical or ready for general use, it does show that quantum technology has reached a point where it can handle problems beyond the reach of classical computing.

1. **Defining Quantum Supremacy**:

- o Quantum supremacy is defined as a situation where a quantum computer performs a task that is computationally infeasible for classical supercomputers. This is often measured in terms of computation time—if a task that would take classical computers thousands of years can be done by a quantum computer in minutes or hours, quantum supremacy is achieved.

- o Importantly, quantum supremacy is achieved with a specific task, typically one designed to be challenging for classical computers but suited for quantum systems.

2. **Why Quantum Supremacy Matters**:

- o **Proof of Quantum Potential**: Quantum supremacy demonstrates the potential of quantum computers to solve complex problems that classical computers cannot manage, validating years of research in the field.

- o **Accelerating Research**: Achieving supremacy encourages further investment and research in quantum computing, as it proves the viability of the technology.

- o **Foundation for Practical Quantum Applications**: While initial tasks that achieve quantum supremacy are often theoretical, the techniques and technologies developed pave the way for practical applications in industries ranging from healthcare to finance to materials science.

Achieving quantum supremacy marks a major milestone in the quantum computing field and signals that we are on the path toward more powerful, general-purpose quantum systems.

Google's Quantum Supremacy Experiment and Its Implications

In 2019, **Google** made headlines by claiming to have achieved quantum supremacy with its 53-qubit quantum processor, **Sycamore**. Google's team reported that Sycamore had completed a complex calculation in about 200 seconds that would take the world's most powerful supercomputer, **Summit**, roughly 10,000 years to solve.

1. **The Experiment**:
   o The experiment performed by Sycamore involved sampling the output of a random quantum circuit. This type of calculation is inherently suited to quantum systems because it relies on the randomness and probabilistic behavior of qubits in a way that classical systems struggle to simulate.
   o Google designed the task specifically to demonstrate quantum supremacy, as it doesn't have immediate

practical applications outside proving the speed and efficiency of quantum computation.

2. **Controversy and Debate**:

   o Google's announcement sparked debate within the scientific community. IBM, a major competitor in the quantum computing space, argued that Google's experiment did not meet the criteria for true quantum supremacy. IBM contended that the task could be solved in a matter of days, rather than thousands of years, using Summit with optimized algorithms.

   o This debate highlights the complexity of defining quantum supremacy and the challenge of creating benchmarks for comparisons between quantum and classical systems.

3. **Implications of Google's Achievement**:

   o **Technological Validation**: Google's experiment provided the first major evidence that quantum computers can surpass classical systems for certain tasks. This validation sparked renewed interest and investment in quantum research.

   o **Catalyst for Quantum Development**: Google's achievement motivated other companies and research institutions to accelerate their own quantum development, intensifying the race to build practical, large-scale quantum computers.

- o **Focus on Practical Quantum Applications**: With quantum supremacy demonstrated, researchers began shifting focus toward practical applications that could benefit industries, such as simulating complex molecules, optimizing logistics, and enhancing machine learning models.

Google's quantum supremacy experiment was a watershed moment for the field, emphasizing the potential of quantum computing and the importance of continued development toward practical applications.

The Race for Practical, Universal Quantum Computing

Quantum supremacy is a major milestone, but the ultimate goal in quantum computing is to develop **practical, universal quantum computers** that can solve a wide range of real-world problems reliably and efficiently. Several key challenges remain:

1. **Scaling Up Quantum Hardware**:
   - o Today's quantum computers have relatively few qubits, often in the range of 50–100. To handle complex, real-world applications, thousands or even millions of qubits may be needed, especially when factoring in the qubits required for error correction.

- o Scaling up to this level requires breakthroughs in qubit stability, coherence time, and inter-qubit connectivity.

2. **Error Correction and Fault Tolerance**:
   - o Errors remain a significant issue in quantum computing, as discussed in the previous chapter. Quantum error correction is essential for creating reliable, fault-tolerant quantum systems, but current error correction techniques are qubit-intensive and challenging to implement on a large scale.
   - o Researchers are working to develop more efficient error correction methods that can bring us closer to practical quantum computing.

3. **Development of Quantum Algorithms**:
   - o Achieving practical, universal quantum computing also depends on developing algorithms that leverage quantum properties to solve useful problems. While promising algorithms like Shor's and Grover's exist, many potential quantum applications remain unexplored.
   - o Quantum algorithm development is a field of ongoing research, with scientists experimenting in areas like quantum machine learning, optimization, and cryptography.

4. **Quantum Cloud Platforms and Accessibility**:

o   Companies like IBM, Google, and Microsoft have begun offering quantum computing through cloud platforms, allowing researchers to experiment with real quantum hardware. These platforms are an essential step in democratizing quantum computing and accelerating development.

o   Cloud-based access to quantum computers allows researchers to run algorithms, test applications, and develop expertise in quantum computing, building a foundation for the next generation of quantum breakthroughs.

The race for practical quantum computing is heating up, with major technology companies, research institutions, and governments working toward the development of universal quantum computers that can tackle complex, real-world problems across various industries.

Real-World Example: Potential Impacts of Quantum Supremacy on Industries

Quantum supremacy opens up possibilities for industries that rely on complex computations, optimization, and simulations that classical computers struggle to handle. Here are some potential impacts:

1. **Pharmaceuticals and Drug Discovery**:
   - o Quantum supremacy could enable breakthroughs in drug discovery by making it possible to simulate complex molecules and biological processes that are currently infeasible to model accurately. Quantum simulations can help researchers design new drugs, predict molecular interactions, and reduce the time and cost of drug development.
   - o For example, quantum computers could potentially simulate proteins and enzymes in ways that classical computers cannot, allowing for the rapid design of effective drugs for diseases like cancer, Alzheimer's, and genetic disorders.

2. **Materials Science and Chemistry**:
   - o Quantum computers could transform materials science by enabling precise simulations of atomic and molecular structures, which would help in designing new materials with desired properties (e.g., superconductors, advanced batteries, and lightweight composites).
   - o In energy production, quantum computing could help develop catalysts for efficient energy storage, carbon capture, and fuel production, contributing to advancements in clean energy and sustainability.

3. **Finance and Cryptography**:

- In finance, quantum computing could optimize complex portfolio management and risk analysis, where large amounts of data and rapid computations are required. Quantum algorithms for optimization, such as Grover's, could allow financial institutions to solve problems faster and with greater accuracy.
- **Quantum cryptography** will also play a crucial role as quantum computers gain power. With the potential to break traditional encryption methods, quantum computers necessitate the development of **quantum-safe cryptographic protocols** to protect sensitive data in finance, government, and communications.

4. **Logistics and Supply Chain Optimization**:
   - Quantum computers could revolutionize logistics by solving complex optimization problems in areas such as transportation, inventory management, and supply chain efficiency. For example, quantum computing could enhance route optimization for delivery networks, minimizing fuel consumption and improving efficiency in real-time.
   - Major industries, such as retail, shipping, and manufacturing, stand to benefit from quantum-accelerated logistics, allowing companies to save on operational costs and enhance service delivery.

5. **Artificial Intelligence and Machine Learning**:
    o Quantum computing has the potential to accelerate machine learning, particularly for complex models and large datasets. Quantum machine learning could make AI systems more accurate, faster, and capable of handling tasks that classical systems struggle with, such as real-time pattern recognition, language translation, and large-scale data analysis.
    o For example, in healthcare, quantum-enhanced machine learning could improve diagnostics by analyzing large sets of medical data, leading to early disease detection and more personalized treatment plans.

The impacts of quantum supremacy on industries are potentially transformative, offering new ways to approach complex problems, reduce operational costs, and accelerate innovation. While practical quantum applications may still be in the future, the field's rapid advancement suggests that industries will likely see tangible benefits within the next decade.

In this chapter, we examined **quantum supremacy**, a significant milestone demonstrating the power of quantum computers to outperform classical supercomputers in specific tasks. We explored the importance of quantum supremacy, discussed Google's 2019 quantum supremacy experiment, and the debate it sparked within the scientific community. We also looked at the race to develop practical, universal quantum computers capable of solving complex, real-world problems and the challenges that remain.

Finally, we explored potential industry impacts of quantum supremacy, particularly in pharmaceuticals, materials science, finance, logistics, and artificial intelligence, where quantum computing could address computational challenges and drive innovation. Achieving quantum supremacy highlights the potential of quantum computing to reshape industries and encourage further investment in the field.

In the next chapter, we'll delve into **quantum-safe cryptography**, exploring how industries can protect sensitive data in a future where quantum computers are powerful enough to break traditional encryption methods.

CHAPTER 15: QUANTUM NETWORKING AND THE QUANTUM INTERNET

Quantum networking is a growing field in quantum computing focused on connecting quantum devices across long distances, enabling the creation of a **quantum internet**. A quantum internet would allow for fundamentally secure communication and interconnected quantum systems. In this chapter, we'll explore the basics of quantum networking, including quantum repeaters and quantum teleportation, the concept of a quantum internet and its potential applications, ongoing research and development in quantum networks, and a real-world example of how a quantum internet could transform cybersecurity.

Basics of Quantum Networking: Quantum Repeaters and Teleportation

Quantum networking relies on quantum principles to transmit information in ways that are secure, instantaneous, and highly resilient against eavesdropping. Two key concepts in quantum networking are **quantum repeaters** and **quantum teleportation**.

1. **Quantum Repeaters**:
   o In classical networks, data can be sent across long distances by using repeaters, which amplify and

retransmit signals. Quantum systems, however, cannot use traditional amplification methods due to the **quantum no-cloning theorem** (the impossibility of copying quantum information without altering it).

- **Quantum repeaters** solve this issue by utilizing **entanglement swapping** and **quantum teleportation** to extend the distance over which quantum states can be transmitted. Quantum repeaters work by creating entangled pairs of particles at various points along a network. These particles relay information without needing to amplify the signal, preserving the integrity of the quantum information over long distances.

- Quantum repeaters are essential for creating large-scale quantum networks and are one of the primary challenges in building a global quantum internet.

2. **Quantum Teleportation**:

- Quantum teleportation is a process that transfers a quantum state from one particle to another over a distance without physically moving the particle itself. Teleportation relies on **quantum entanglement**, which links two particles in such a way that the state of one particle instantaneously affects the other, no matter the distance between them.

- o In quantum networking, teleportation is used to transmit quantum information between network nodes by creating entangled pairs of particles at each node. The information encoded in one particle can be "teleported" to the entangled particle at a distant location, transferring quantum states securely and instantaneously.

Together, quantum repeaters and teleportation form the foundation of quantum networking, enabling long-distance quantum communication by leveraging the principles of entanglement and teleportation without violating the no-cloning theorem.

The Concept of a Quantum Internet and Its Applications

A **quantum internet** would function much like today's internet but with the added benefit of **quantum-level security** and **instantaneous communication** enabled by quantum entanglement. The quantum internet would connect quantum devices, sensors, and computers across a global network, with various applications across industries.

1. **Unbreakable Security**:
   - o One of the main applications of a quantum internet is secure communication. Quantum networks inherently detect any eavesdropping attempts due to

the **disturbance** caused when someone tries to intercept a quantum transmission.

o By leveraging **quantum key distribution (QKD)**, a quantum internet could facilitate secure exchange of cryptographic keys for encrypted communication, creating a level of data protection that is theoretically immune to both classical and quantum attacks.

2. **Interconnected Quantum Computers**:

o A quantum internet would connect quantum computers worldwide, enabling collaborative computation and **distributed quantum processing**. This could allow multiple quantum computers to work together on complex problems, share computational workloads, and enable new applications in fields like materials science, drug discovery, and artificial intelligence.

o Interconnected quantum systems could lead to powerful advancements in fields that require extensive data processing and large-scale simulations.

3. **Quantum Sensor Networks**:

o Quantum sensors, which are highly sensitive devices that can detect minute changes in magnetic fields, gravity, or other physical forces, could be interconnected through a quantum network. This network could have applications in fields like **environmental monitoring, medical diagnostics**, and **national security** by providing real-time, accurate data with unparalleled sensitivity.

o A quantum internet could enable sensor networks that improve earthquake detection, monitor ecological changes, or provide early detection of diseases through advanced diagnostics.

4. **Enhanced Scientific Research**:

o By connecting quantum computers, researchers could use quantum simulations to study phenomena like **quantum mechanics, black holes**, and **quantum gravity**, which are difficult to model on classical computers. The quantum internet could provide the bandwidth and connectivity needed for large-scale scientific projects, enabling distributed research on a global scale.

A quantum internet would go far beyond the capabilities of today's classical networks, offering enhanced security, connectivity, and computational potential.

Current Research and Development in Quantum Networks
Research into quantum networks is rapidly advancing, with academic institutions, government agencies, and technology companies all working on the necessary hardware and infrastructure

to build a quantum internet. Here are some major developments and initiatives:

1. **Quantum Network Testbeds**:
   o Governments and research institutions worldwide are investing in quantum network testbeds to advance quantum communication technologies. For example:
     - **The Quantum Internet Alliance (QIA)**, a European initiative, aims to build a European quantum network by developing quantum repeaters and teleportation protocols.
     - **China's Quantum Experiments at Space Scale (QUESS)** project demonstrated secure quantum communication by sending entangled particles from a satellite to ground stations, a major step toward building a space-based quantum internet.
     - The **U.S. Department of Energy (DOE)** has also established a national quantum internet research program, aiming to create a quantum network that spans the United States.

2. **Quantum Repeaters and Infrastructure**:
   o Research is ongoing to develop effective quantum repeaters that can extend the reach of quantum

communication. Companies and research institutions are working on the engineering challenges required to develop repeaters that can preserve entanglement over long distances with high fidelity.

o Additionally, infrastructure developments, such as fiber-optic cables tailored for quantum signals and specialized nodes to manage quantum entanglement, are being designed and tested.

3. **Quantum Cryptographic Protocols**:

o As part of quantum network research, scientists are also developing quantum cryptographic protocols that can leverage quantum networks for secure communication. Protocols like **quantum key distribution (QKD)** and **quantum-secure multi-party computation** are advancing in tandem with network development, ensuring that the quantum internet will provide unprecedented security for data transmission.

These research efforts are pushing quantum networks closer to reality, with initial implementations likely to appear in the next decade as testbed results and prototypes evolve into more advanced, scalable networks.

Real-World Example: How a Quantum Internet Could Change Cybersecurity

One of the most promising applications of a quantum internet is in **cybersecurity**, where it has the potential to fundamentally change how we secure sensitive data.

1. **Problem**:
   o Today's cybersecurity relies on encryption methods like RSA, which could be broken by powerful quantum computers in the future. This risk makes secure communication increasingly challenging, as traditional encryption methods may no longer be effective against quantum attacks.

2. **Solution: Quantum Key Distribution (QKD)**:
   o A quantum internet could make secure communication possible through **Quantum Key Distribution (QKD)**. QKD uses quantum properties to establish cryptographic keys that are impossible to intercept without detection. If an eavesdropper attempts to intercept a QKD transmission, the act of measuring the qubits will disturb their state, alerting both sender and receiver to a security breach.
   o With QKD, sensitive information such as financial transactions, government communications, and personal data could be secured, ensuring that only intended parties have access.

3. **Implementing Quantum-Secured Communications**:

o Consider a bank sending sensitive financial data to another branch over a quantum internet. The bank could use QKD to establish a shared cryptographic key between the two branches. Once the key is exchanged, all communications would be encrypted with it.

o Even if a malicious actor intercepts the transmission, they would be unable to decipher the data because any interception attempt would introduce errors detectable by the communicating parties. This makes quantum-secured communications highly resilient against interception.

4. **Impact on Data Privacy and National Security**:

o A quantum internet could be particularly valuable in fields where data privacy is essential, such as healthcare, finance, and government. For instance, healthcare providers could securely transmit patient records and medical data, while financial institutions could protect sensitive financial transactions from potential threats.

o National security agencies could use the quantum internet to communicate without fear of interception, ensuring that sensitive information remains confidential even in the face of advanced cyber threats.

By creating secure, resilient communication channels, a quantum internet could address pressing cybersecurity concerns in the digital age, offering a new standard of data protection and privacy.

In this chapter, we explored **quantum networking** and the potential for a **quantum internet**, which promises to revolutionize secure communication and data sharing. We covered the basics of quantum networking technologies, including **quantum repeaters** and **quantum teleportation**, which enable long-distance quantum communication without violating the no-cloning theorem. We then examined the concept of a quantum internet, highlighting its applications in security, interconnected quantum computing, and scientific research.

We also discussed ongoing research and development efforts in quantum networking, including initiatives from government agencies and research institutions aimed at creating the necessary infrastructure. Through a real-world example, we explored how a quantum internet could transform cybersecurity, enabling unbreakable encryption and secure communication for sensitive data across industries.

In the next chapter, we'll dive into **quantum-safe cryptography**, which aims to develop encryption methods resistant to both classical and quantum attacks, preparing us for a future where quantum computers might threaten traditional encryption.

CHAPTER 16: BUILDING A CAREER IN QUANTUM COMPUTING

As **quantum computing** continues to advance, demand for skilled professionals in this field is growing rapidly. Building a career in quantum computing requires a unique blend of skills, spanning physics, mathematics, programming, and an understanding of quantum mechanics. In this chapter, we'll explore the essential skills needed for a quantum computing career, look at various roles within the field, recommend academic programs and certifications, and examine the career path of a quantum computing professional as a real-world example.

Essential Skills for Quantum Computing Careers

To excel in quantum computing, a strong foundation in several core disciplines is required:

1. **Mathematics**:
   - Quantum computing relies heavily on advanced mathematics, particularly **linear algebra** (for understanding vector spaces, matrices, and quantum states), **probability theory** (to interpret quantum measurements and outcomes), and **complex numbers** (to represent quantum states).

    o **Discrete mathematics** and **group theory** are also useful, as they provide insights into algorithm design and the behavior of quantum systems.

2. **Physics**:

    o **Quantum mechanics** is at the heart of quantum computing, and an understanding of its fundamental principles—such as superposition, entanglement, and wave functions—is essential.

    o Knowledge of **electromagnetic theory** and **solid-state physics** can also be beneficial, especially for those working on quantum hardware, where the behavior of particles at the atomic level affects quantum device design and performance.

3. **Computer Science and Programming**:

    o Quantum computing requires proficiency in programming, particularly in languages and frameworks designed for quantum systems. Familiarity with **Qiskit** (Python-based quantum computing library), **Cirq** (Google's quantum framework), and **Q#** (Microsoft's quantum programming language) is highly recommended.

    o A solid understanding of **classical algorithms** and **data structures** is essential for those developing quantum algorithms, as it provides a foundation to understand how quantum algorithms can offer advantages over classical approaches.

4. **Algorithm Design and Optimization**:

   o Quantum algorithms, like Shor's for factoring and Grover's for searching, are unique in structure. Understanding algorithm design and optimization allows professionals to develop new quantum algorithms and optimize existing ones.

   o Knowledge of **complexity theory** and **quantum information theory** is also useful, as it helps in understanding the limits and capabilities of quantum computing.

5. **Research and Analytical Skills**:

   o Quantum computing is a rapidly evolving field, requiring professionals to stay updated on the latest research and developments. Strong research skills are crucial, especially for those interested in developing new technologies or advancing quantum computing theory.

   o Analytical skills are essential for debugging, optimizing, and interpreting results from quantum experiments and simulations.

These skills provide a comprehensive foundation for various roles in quantum computing, from theoretical research to hardware development and software engineering.

Quantum Computing Roles: Research Scientist, Engineer, Software Developer, and More

Quantum computing offers a range of roles that vary based on skill set and focus. Here are some common positions in the field:

1. **Quantum Research Scientist**:
   - o **Responsibilities**: Conduct theoretical and applied research to develop new quantum algorithms, study quantum information theory, and contribute to quantum physics research.
   - o **Skills**: Strong background in quantum mechanics, linear algebra, and quantum algorithms. Research skills and experience in academic or lab settings are essential.
   - o **Ideal for**: Individuals interested in the science and theory of quantum computing, often working in universities, government labs, or private research institutions.

2. **Quantum Software Developer**:
   - o **Responsibilities**: Design, develop, and optimize software for quantum computers, including quantum algorithms, libraries, and simulations. Quantum

software developers often work with frameworks like Qiskit, Cirq, and Q#.

- o **Skills**: Programming skills in Python, experience with quantum libraries, understanding of quantum algorithms, and knowledge of classical computer science.

- o **Ideal for**: Programmers interested in the practical applications of quantum computing, often working in tech companies, research organizations, or startups.

3. **Quantum Hardware Engineer**:

- o **Responsibilities**: Design and develop quantum computing hardware, such as quantum processors and qubit systems. This role may involve creating superconducting circuits, trapped ion systems, or other quantum technologies.

- o **Skills**: Solid-state physics, electromagnetism, cryogenics, and materials science. Hands-on experience with laboratory equipment is often necessary.

- o **Ideal for**: Engineers with a strong physics background who are interested in building and improving the physical components of quantum computers, often working in hardware-focused companies or research labs.

4. **Quantum Algorithm Developer**:

- o **Responsibilities**: Develop new quantum algorithms or optimize existing ones for specific applications, such as cryptography, optimization, or machine learning.
- o **Skills**: Advanced knowledge of quantum mechanics, quantum information theory, and algorithm design. Familiarity with mathematical software and simulation tools.
- o **Ideal for**: Those with a strong theoretical background and an interest in applying quantum principles to solve complex computational problems.

5. **Quantum Network Engineer**:
   - o **Responsibilities**: Design and implement quantum communication systems, such as quantum key distribution networks and quantum repeaters.
   - o **Skills**: Quantum mechanics, networking, cryptography, and knowledge of quantum communication protocols.
   - o **Ideal for**: Professionals interested in the intersection of quantum computing and secure communications, often working in telecommunications, defense, or research institutions.

6. **Quantum Machine Learning Scientist**:
   - o **Responsibilities**: Apply quantum computing to machine learning problems, such as training models,

feature selection, and optimization tasks. Develop quantum-enhanced machine learning algorithms.

- o **Skills**: Machine learning, quantum computing, statistics, and algorithm design.
- o **Ideal for**: Data scientists or machine learning engineers interested in exploring quantum computing's impact on AI and data science.

Each role offers unique contributions to the field, making it possible for professionals with diverse backgrounds to participate in advancing quantum computing technology.

Recommended Academic Programs and Certifications

The interdisciplinary nature of quantum computing makes it essential to pursue targeted education and training. Here are some recommended academic programs and certifications:

1. **Academic Degrees**:
   - o **Bachelor's Degree**: Fields such as physics, electrical engineering, computer science, or applied mathematics provide foundational knowledge in relevant disciplines. An undergraduate degree is often the first step for those pursuing a career in quantum computing.
   - o **Master's Degree**: Graduate programs in **quantum information science**, **quantum engineering**,

computer science, or **physics** allow students to gain specialized knowledge and engage in research projects.

o **PhD Programs**: For research-intensive roles, a PhD in quantum physics, quantum information, or related fields is typically required. Many research institutions and universities offer advanced research opportunities for doctoral students.

2. **Certifications**:

o **IBM Quantum Computing Certificate** (via Qiskit): IBM offers free courses and certifications through its Qiskit platform, providing hands-on experience with quantum programming and simulations.

o **MIT xPro's Quantum Computing Fundamentals**: This online course introduces quantum computing fundamentals, covering topics such as quantum mechanics, quantum algorithms, and applications.

o **Quantum Computing Certification by the University of Toronto**: An introductory course available on platforms like Coursera, which covers quantum computing basics, programming, and applications.

3. **Workshops and Bootcamps**:

o **Qiskit Global Summer School**: Hosted by IBM, this program provides an intensive two-week course on quantum computing fundamentals and programming.

- **Quantum Machine Learning Bootcamps**: Programs focused on the intersection of quantum computing and machine learning, offered by organizations like Xanadu and Google.

These programs and certifications allow aspiring quantum computing professionals to build essential skills and gain hands-on experience with quantum technology.

Real-World Example: Profile of a Quantum Computing Professional and Their Career Path
Profile: Dr. Elena Thompson, Quantum Algorithm Developer

1. **Educational Background**:
   - **Bachelor's Degree**: Dr. Thompson began her journey with a bachelor's degree in physics, where she developed a strong foundation in quantum mechanics and linear algebra. Her early interest in quantum theory motivated her to pursue a career in the field.
   - **Master's Degree**: She completed a master's degree in quantum information science, focusing on quantum algorithms and their applications. During her graduate studies, she interned at a tech company,

gaining practical experience in quantum programming with Qiskit.

- o **PhD in Quantum Information Theory**: To further her research capabilities, Dr. Thompson pursued a PhD, specializing in quantum algorithm development for optimization problems. Her dissertation involved designing quantum algorithms for efficient data search, leading to several publications in respected journals.

2. **Early Career**:

- o After completing her PhD, Dr. Thompson worked as a postdoctoral researcher at a national laboratory, where she contributed to projects involving quantum algorithm design for government applications. Her research on Grover's algorithm and optimization techniques gained recognition, and she began speaking at conferences.

3. **Transition to Industry**:

- o Dr. Thompson was offered a role as a **Quantum Algorithm Developer** at a technology company working on quantum computing solutions for logistics and finance. Her job involved designing and implementing algorithms to optimize supply chains and financial portfolios, using quantum computing frameworks like Qiskit and custom simulation tools.

4. **Current Role and Projects**:

- Today, Dr. Thompson leads a team of researchers focused on applying quantum algorithms to machine learning models, exploring ways quantum computing can accelerate training times and improve data processing.

- Her day-to-day tasks include collaborating with quantum hardware engineers to optimize algorithm compatibility, conducting simulations, and presenting findings to potential clients in industries like healthcare and finance.

5. **Impact and Advice**:

- Dr. Thompson's work has contributed to advancements in quantum optimization and machine learning. She advises aspiring quantum computing professionals to focus on interdisciplinary skills, emphasizing the importance of understanding both theoretical concepts and practical applications.

- Her advice: "Build a strong foundation in physics and math, but also become proficient in quantum programming languages like Qiskit. The quantum field is still young, and there's a lot of room for innovation and discovery."

Dr. Thompson's career path showcases the diverse opportunities in quantum computing and highlights the importance of combining theoretical knowledge with practical experience.

In this chapter, we explored the skills, roles, and educational paths essential for building a career in **quantum computing**. Key skills include proficiency in mathematics, quantum mechanics, computer science, and programming. We examined several career paths, including **research scientists**, **software developers**, **hardware engineers**, and **quantum algorithm developers**, each requiring unique expertise within the field.

We also recommended academic programs and certifications to help aspiring professionals gain foundational knowledge and hands-on experience. Through the example of Dr. Elena Thompson's career, we saw how a quantum computing professional can progress from academia to industry, contributing to advancements in quantum algorithms and their applications.

In the next chapter, we'll explore **ethical considerations and challenges in quantum computing**, addressing the potential societal impacts and the responsibility of professionals in this transformative field.

CHAPTER 17: QUANTUM COMPUTING ETHICS AND SECURITY

As **quantum computing** technology advances, it brings both unprecedented opportunities and significant ethical and security concerns. Quantum computing has the potential to reshape industries and solve complex problems, but it also poses a threat to traditional cryptographic systems, which could impact global security and privacy. In this chapter, we'll examine key ethical considerations in quantum computing, discuss the potential quantum threats to classical cryptography and data protection, explore how we can prepare for a post-quantum world, and provide a real-world example illustrating the importance of developing quantum-safe encryption.

Ethical Considerations with Quantum Computing (Privacy, Security)

Quantum computing has a range of ethical implications, especially concerning **privacy** and **security**. Here are some of the major ethical considerations:

1. **Privacy**:
    o Quantum computers' potential to break widely used encryption systems poses a significant privacy risk. If quantum computing becomes capable of

decrypting sensitive data, personal and corporate information could be exposed to unauthorized access, undermining individual privacy and organizational confidentiality.

o Governments, corporations, and individuals store vast amounts of sensitive information, from financial records to personal communications. Quantum technology could disrupt existing privacy protections if ethical safeguards are not implemented.

2. **Security**:

o Quantum computers could render current security systems obsolete by breaking encryption schemes like RSA and ECC (Elliptic Curve Cryptography), which are foundational for securing digital communications and protecting data.

o Without secure encryption alternatives, critical infrastructure, government communications, financial transactions, and even online interactions could become vulnerable to cyberattacks. This security vulnerability raises concerns about data theft, surveillance, and global cybersecurity.

3. **Potential for Misuse**:

o Like all powerful technologies, quantum computing has the potential to be misused if it falls into the wrong hands. Quantum-powered cyberattacks could compromise national security, economic stability, and personal privacy on a massive scale.

o Quantum computing also has implications for artificial intelligence, as quantum algorithms could supercharge machine learning capabilities. This power raises concerns about the ethical use of AI, particularly in areas such as surveillance, autonomous systems, and decision-making processes.

4. **Access and Equity**:

o Quantum computing technology is currently accessible only to a limited number of governments, corporations, and research institutions with significant resources. This limited access could widen the digital divide, favoring nations and organizations that can afford to invest in quantum technologies.

o Ensuring equitable access to quantum computing and developing policies to prevent monopolies on quantum technology are important ethical considerations, particularly in applications with broad social or economic impact.

Addressing these ethical considerations will require collaboration among policymakers, technologists, ethicists, and organizations to ensure that quantum computing serves the public good.

Quantum Threats to Classical Cryptography and Data Protection

One of the most pressing concerns regarding quantum computing is its ability to break classical cryptographic methods that are currently used to secure data worldwide.

1. **The Vulnerability of Classical Encryption**:
   - Classical encryption methods like RSA and ECC rely on the difficulty of mathematical problems such as integer factorization and discrete logarithms. While these problems are hard for classical computers to solve, quantum algorithms, specifically **Shor's algorithm**, can solve them efficiently, posing a direct threat to encryption systems that secure everything from emails to financial transactions.
   - **RSA encryption**, for example, relies on the difficulty of factoring large numbers into primes. Shor's algorithm, however, can factor these large numbers exponentially faster than classical methods, allowing a quantum computer to break RSA encryption with relative ease as soon as the technology becomes scalable.

2. **Implications for Data Protection**:
   - Once a sufficiently powerful quantum computer is built, it could potentially decrypt any data that has been encrypted with classical encryption methods.

This capability threatens not only current communications but also **"data in transit"** (data being sent over networks) and **"data at rest"** (stored data).

o Sensitive information stored today under classical encryption could become vulnerable in the future if encrypted using classical methods alone. This possibility is a concern for long-term data storage, especially for industries handling highly confidential data, such as healthcare, finance, and government.

3. **The Need for Quantum-Safe Cryptography**:

o To prepare for quantum computing's impact on cryptography, researchers are developing **quantum-safe (or post-quantum) cryptographic algorithms** that are resistant to both classical and quantum attacks.

o Quantum-safe encryption methods, such as **lattice-based cryptography** and **hash-based cryptography**, are designed to remain secure even in the face of quantum decryption capabilities. These algorithms are undergoing testing and standardization to protect against quantum threats and provide an alternative to existing encryption systems.

The transition to quantum-safe cryptography is crucial to preserving data security and privacy as quantum computing capabilities continue to develop.

Preparing for a Post-Quantum World

Organizations, governments, and individuals must take proactive steps to prepare for the potential impact of quantum computing on data security. Here are key strategies for preparing for a post-quantum world:

1. **Transitioning to Quantum-Safe Encryption**:
    - Organizations should begin integrating quantum-safe cryptographic methods to protect sensitive data. The National Institute of Standards and Technology (**NIST**) has been working on standardizing post-quantum cryptographic algorithms, providing guidance on adopting these new protocols.
    - Implementing quantum-safe encryption will ensure that data remains protected even as quantum computing progresses, reducing the risk of a "quantum cryptography apocalypse," where classical encryption becomes obsolete.

2. **Hybrid Encryption Solutions**:
    - Until quantum-safe encryption standards are fully established, organizations can adopt hybrid encryption solutions that combine classical and

quantum-safe cryptographic methods. Hybrid systems provide a buffer by protecting data with both classical and quantum-safe protocols, allowing for a gradual transition.

- o Hybrid encryption is particularly useful for securing long-term data storage and highly sensitive communications, as it provides protection against potential quantum attacks while remaining compatible with current systems.

3. **Assessing and Updating Security Policies**:

- o Governments and businesses should assess their current encryption policies, evaluate potential quantum vulnerabilities, and update their security protocols accordingly.
- o Security teams should also stay informed about advancements in quantum-safe cryptography and begin preparing for large-scale encryption updates as quantum-safe algorithms are standardized.

4. **Investment in Quantum Research and Workforce Development**:

- o Preparing for a post-quantum world will require a skilled workforce proficient in quantum-safe encryption, quantum algorithms, and cybersecurity. Governments and educational institutions are investing in training programs and research to build this workforce.

o By investing in research and workforce development, countries and companies can position themselves to adapt to the changes that quantum computing will bring, ensuring secure systems and a competitive edge in the post-quantum era.

Transitioning to a post-quantum world will take time and resources, but it is essential for protecting data and maintaining cybersecurity in the face of advancing quantum technology.

Real-World Example: The Importance of Developing Quantum-Safe Encryption

Scenario: A Financial Institution Prepares for Quantum Security Risks

1. **Problem**:

o A large financial institution handles sensitive customer information, including account details, transaction records, and personal data. This data is secured using classical encryption methods such as RSA, which could be compromised if a powerful quantum computer becomes capable of breaking RSA encryption.

2. **Solution: Transition to Quantum-Safe Encryption**:

   o To mitigate the risk, the institution adopts a proactive approach to transition to quantum-safe encryption methods. After evaluating its data security requirements, the institution implements a hybrid encryption system that combines RSA with a lattice-based quantum-safe cryptographic protocol.

   o The institution follows the **NIST standards** for post-quantum cryptography, ensuring that the encryption methods they adopt are robust against both classical and quantum attacks.

3. **Implementation**:

   o The IT department creates a roadmap for a full migration to quantum-safe encryption, starting with the most sensitive data and high-priority systems. They deploy hybrid encryption solutions to protect customer data in transit and at rest, providing a double layer of security.

   o Additionally, the institution trains its cybersecurity staff on quantum-safe encryption techniques, enabling them to maintain secure systems as technology evolves.

4. **Outcome**:

   o By transitioning to quantum-safe encryption, the financial institution ensures that customer data remains secure, protecting against potential quantum threats. This proactive approach also gives the institution a competitive advantage, as customers can trust that their data is protected with state-of-the-art encryption.

- o Furthermore, the institution's move to quantum-safe encryption serves as an example for other organizations, highlighting the importance of preparing for quantum technology's impact on cybersecurity.

This example underscores the critical role of quantum-safe encryption in safeguarding data, especially for industries with high security and privacy requirements, such as finance, healthcare, and government.

In this chapter, we explored the ethical and security considerations surrounding **quantum computing**, focusing on issues related to **privacy** and **data protection**. We discussed how quantum computing's potential to break classical encryption methods poses a threat to current cryptographic systems, impacting global security and individual privacy. The chapter highlighted the need for quantum-safe cryptography as a solution to protect data in a post-quantum world.

We also examined key strategies for preparing for quantum threats, such as transitioning to quantum-safe encryption, implementing hybrid encryption solutions, and investing in quantum research and workforce development. Through the real-world example of a financial institution preparing for quantum security risks, we saw the importance of adopting quantum-safe encryption to ensure data protection in an era where quantum computing capabilities may challenge existing security measures.

In the next chapter, we'll discuss **quantum computing's potential environmental impact**, exploring both the positive and negative implications of scaling up quantum technology on energy consumption and resource use.

CHAPTER 18: QUANTUM COMPUTING IN INDUSTRY

As quantum computing technology matures, industries are beginning to explore its potential applications, preparing for the impact it could have on solving complex, large-scale problems that classical computers cannot efficiently address. Sectors like **finance**, **healthcare**, and **energy** are leading the charge, collaborating with quantum computing companies and forming consortia to develop quantum solutions. In this chapter, we'll explore how various industries are adopting quantum computing, discuss key quantum consortia and collaborations, and examine real-world case studies of companies leveraging quantum technology today.

How Industries are Preparing for and Using Quantum Computing
Industries are preparing for quantum computing by investing in research, training, and collaborative projects. Here's a look at some of the major sectors and how they're using or preparing to use quantum technology:

1. **Finance**:
    - **Problem**: The finance industry deals with complex data and optimization challenges, from portfolio management to risk assessment and fraud detection.

- o **Quantum Applications**: Quantum computers offer significant potential for **portfolio optimization**, **derivative pricing**, and **risk analysis**. Quantum algorithms can handle these large datasets more efficiently, providing faster and more accurate results than classical methods.
- o **Example**: Several financial institutions, including JPMorgan Chase and Goldman Sachs, are working with quantum computing companies to explore quantum algorithms for portfolio optimization and pricing complex financial instruments.

2. **Healthcare and Pharmaceuticals**:

- o **Problem**: Developing new drugs and treatments is a costly, time-consuming process that requires precise molecular simulations and testing.
- o **Quantum Applications**: Quantum computers can simulate molecular interactions at the quantum level, allowing pharmaceutical companies to identify promising drug candidates faster and reduce the need for physical trials. Quantum computing also has potential applications in personalized medicine, helping doctors tailor treatments based on complex patient data.
- o **Example**: Pharmaceutical companies like Pfizer and Roche are working with quantum computing firms to

speed up drug discovery and optimize chemical reactions.

3. **Energy**:

   o **Problem**: The energy sector faces challenges in optimizing energy production, managing grid infrastructure, and developing new energy storage solutions.

   o **Quantum Applications**: Quantum computing could help in designing more efficient solar cells, improving battery materials, and optimizing power grids for better efficiency. Quantum simulations could enable more accurate models for fuel production and carbon capture technologies, contributing to sustainability goals.

   o **Example**: Companies like ExxonMobil and BP are investing in quantum research for optimizing energy production and exploring new materials for batteries and sustainable energy solutions.

4. **Logistics and Supply Chain**:

   o **Problem**: Large-scale logistics and supply chain management involves complex routing and inventory optimization, especially in global operations.

   o **Quantum Applications**: Quantum algorithms, particularly for optimization and combinatorial problems, could streamline supply chains, enhance route optimization, and reduce costs associated with warehousing and transportation.

- o **Example**: DHL and Volkswagen are exploring quantum computing applications in logistics to optimize delivery routes and reduce fuel consumption.

5. **Cybersecurity**:

- o **Problem**: The threat posed by quantum computers to current encryption systems has prompted industries to adopt quantum-safe cryptographic methods.

- o **Quantum Applications**: Quantum key distribution (QKD) and quantum-safe encryption protocols are being developed to secure data and communications. Companies are working on encryption solutions that will withstand potential quantum attacks.

- o **Example**: Telecommunications companies like BT and Verizon are investigating quantum cryptography solutions to ensure the security of communications in the post-quantum era.

Industries are increasingly investing in quantum technology to gain a competitive edge, improve efficiency, and future-proof their systems against potential quantum computing impacts.

Quantum Computing Consortia and Collaborations

Quantum computing development is often a collaborative effort, involving consortia, partnerships, and alliances among tech companies, research institutions, and industry stakeholders. These collaborations accelerate research, establish standards, and facilitate knowledge sharing:

1. **IBM Quantum Network**:
   - IBM has created a network of companies, research institutions, and universities that have access to its quantum computers via cloud services. Members include JPMorgan Chase, Daimler, and Mitsubishi Chemical. The IBM Quantum Network fosters collaboration on real-world applications and supports research to advance quantum technology.

2. **Quantum Economic Development Consortium (QED-C)**:
   - The QED-C, initiated by the U.S. government, is a consortium of over 150 companies, universities, and national labs working to advance quantum research and industry. QED-C's goal is to support quantum workforce development, supply chain initiatives, and collaboration among quantum stakeholders in the United States.

3. **Quantum Computing and AI Collaboration (Google, NASA, and Universities)**:

- o Google has partnered with NASA, academic institutions, and other research organizations to push quantum research forward. Google's Quantum AI Lab collaborates with NASA Ames and other partners on experiments and quantum algorithm development.

4. **European Quantum Industry Consortium (QuIC):**
   - o The QuIC is a European initiative to bring together stakeholders from across the EU's quantum technology landscape. By promoting collaboration and funding research, the QuIC aims to establish Europe as a leading hub for quantum computing development.

5. **National Quantum Initiative (NQI) and Quantum Hubs:**
   - o In the U.S., the National Quantum Initiative Act was passed to accelerate quantum research and development through federal funding. This initiative established quantum research hubs across the country, each focused on specific areas, such as quantum networking, simulation, and sensing.

These consortia and partnerships encourage collaboration and knowledge sharing, essential for scaling up quantum technology and accelerating its adoption in industry.

Real-World Case Studies: Companies Using Quantum Computing Today

Several companies are actively experimenting with quantum computing to solve industry-specific problems. Here are some real-world examples of companies leading the way in quantum computing applications:

1. **JPMorgan Chase (Finance)**:
   - **Application**: JPMorgan Chase has been working on quantum algorithms for **portfolio optimization** and **financial modeling**. The bank is using IBM's quantum computing services to develop algorithms that can calculate risk and price derivatives more efficiently than classical methods.
   - **Goal**: By investing in quantum algorithms for financial analysis, JPMorgan Chase aims to improve the speed and accuracy of its trading and investment decisions. The company has also explored quantum cryptography to protect sensitive financial data.

2. **Volkswagen (Automotive and Logistics)**:
   - **Application**: Volkswagen is leveraging quantum computing to tackle optimization problems in logistics and traffic management. In collaboration with D-Wave, Volkswagen developed a **traffic flow optimization** system that reduces congestion by

optimizing bus and car routes based on quantum algorithms.

- o **Goal**: Volkswagen's aim is to improve urban traffic systems, reduce fuel consumption, and optimize transportation logistics. The company is also exploring quantum computing for battery materials development in electric vehicles.

3. **Pfizer (Pharmaceuticals)**:

- o **Application**: Pfizer is working on quantum computing applications for **drug discovery** and **molecular simulation**. The company partners with IBM to explore how quantum simulations can accelerate the identification of new drug candidates by predicting molecular interactions with high accuracy.

- o **Goal**: Pfizer's goal is to shorten the drug development timeline and increase the success rate of new drug trials. By using quantum simulations, Pfizer hopes to reduce the cost and time required to bring new treatments to market.

4. **ExxonMobil (Energy)**:

- o **Application**: ExxonMobil has collaborated with IBM to explore quantum computing applications in energy optimization, including simulations for **carbon capture** and **fuel production**. Quantum algorithms could allow ExxonMobil to improve the efficiency of chemical processes, reducing energy consumption and carbon emissions.

o **Goal**: ExxonMobil's objective is to support sustainability by developing greener energy production methods. The company is exploring quantum computing as a tool for advancing climate-friendly technologies.

5. **DHL (Logistics)**:

o **Application**: DHL has been experimenting with quantum computing to optimize supply chain logistics, including **route optimization** and **inventory management**. In collaboration with Fujitsu, DHL uses quantum-inspired algorithms to improve delivery efficiency and reduce operational costs.

o **Goal**: By implementing quantum-based optimization, DHL aims to enhance the reliability and speed of its global logistics operations, reduce fuel consumption, and cut overall costs.

6. **BBVA (Banking)**:

o **Application**: BBVA, a global bank based in Spain, is researching quantum computing applications for **fraud detection** and **risk analysis**. By using quantum machine learning algorithms, BBVA can analyze large transaction datasets to detect anomalies more accurately.

- o **Goal**: BBVA's goal is to improve its fraud detection systems, enhance cybersecurity, and develop faster, more efficient models for credit risk analysis.

These case studies highlight how companies across industries are actively testing and implementing quantum technology to tackle complex problems, improve efficiency, and gain competitive advantages.

In this chapter, we explored how **quantum computing** is being adopted by various industries, including finance, healthcare, energy, logistics, and cybersecurity. We discussed how companies in these sectors are investing in quantum technology to solve industry-specific problems, from optimizing portfolios to discovering new drugs and improving logistics.

We also examined the role of quantum computing consortia and collaborations, such as the IBM Quantum Network, Quantum Economic Development Consortium, and the European Quantum Industry Consortium, in advancing quantum technology. These partnerships facilitate knowledge sharing, support workforce development, and drive research into practical applications.

Through real-world case studies, we saw how companies like JPMorgan Chase, Volkswagen, Pfizer, ExxonMobil, DHL, and

BBVA are using quantum computing to gain insights, optimize operations, and develop new technologies that can address complex challenges. These case studies demonstrate the tangible impact that quantum computing is beginning to have across industries.

In the next chapter, we'll discuss **the environmental impact of quantum computing**, exploring the energy requirements, sustainability concerns, and potential environmental benefits of scaling up quantum technology.

CHAPTER 19: THE CHALLENGES FACING QUANTUM COMPUTING

Quantum computing has made impressive progress, but it still faces significant challenges before it can become a reliable and widely-used technology. From technical and physical limitations to infrastructure and scalability issues, quantum computing's path forward is filled with hurdles that require innovative solutions. In this chapter, we'll explore the primary challenges facing quantum computing, including technical, physical, and practical barriers; funding and infrastructure needs; ongoing research efforts; and potential solutions. We'll also use a real-world analogy to compare quantum computing's current stage to that of early classical computing, providing context for the journey ahead.

Technical, Physical, and Practical Barriers to Quantum Computing

Quantum computing faces a range of barriers that stem from both the nature of quantum mechanics and the technological requirements to operate quantum devices:

1. **Qubit Stability (Decoherence)**:
   o Qubits are highly sensitive to environmental noise and interference. Even slight temperature variations,

electromagnetic fields, or vibration can cause **decoherence**, where qubits lose their quantum state. This loss of state disrupts calculations and limits the reliability of quantum operations.

o Maintaining **coherence time** (the duration a qubit remains stable) is a significant challenge. As quantum circuits grow more complex, preserving coherence across many qubits becomes increasingly difficult.

2. **Error Rates and Quantum Error Correction**:

o Quantum computers are prone to errors due to the fragile nature of qubits and the precision required in quantum gate operations. **Error rates** in quantum systems are currently high, and existing error correction methods require multiple physical qubits to encode a single logical qubit, creating substantial overhead.

o Developing scalable **quantum error correction** methods that do not require extensive qubit resources is essential for building larger and more reliable quantum systems.

3. **Scalability of Qubits**:

o Today's quantum computers typically have a few dozen to a few hundred qubits, but large-scale quantum computations require thousands or millions of qubits. Scaling up while maintaining connectivity, coherence, and error correction is a major hurdle.

o Physical layouts, such as the spacing and connectivity of qubits on a chip, become more challenging as the number of qubits grows, especially in systems like superconducting qubits and trapped ions.

4. **Cooling Requirements**:

o Superconducting qubits, used by IBM and Google, operate at temperatures near absolute zero, requiring advanced cryogenic cooling systems. These systems are costly, complex, and consume a large amount of energy, making it difficult to scale up quantum computing infrastructure sustainably.

o Other qubit types, such as photonic qubits, offer alternatives, but each technology has unique requirements that add complexity to the scaling process.

5. **Measurement and Readout Challenges**:

o Measuring qubit states without disturbing the quantum computation is another difficult task. The act of measurement collapses a qubit's quantum state, and if not done with precision, it can introduce errors.

   o Developing more precise and non-intrusive readout techniques is necessary to obtain accurate results from quantum computers.

6. **Programming and Software Limitations**:

   o Quantum programming languages and development environments are still in their infancy compared to classical programming. Developers must contend with a steep learning curve, as well as limited tools and libraries.

   o To broaden quantum computing's accessibility, more robust software ecosystems, user-friendly programming environments, and intuitive debugging tools are needed.

These barriers illustrate that quantum computing is still in the experimental stage, with many challenges requiring breakthroughs in hardware, materials science, and software development.

Funding, Infrastructure, and Scalability Challenges

Building scalable quantum computing infrastructure requires significant investment in both financial and physical resources:

1. **High Cost of Development**:

   o Quantum research and development require substantial funding due to the high cost of equipment, materials, and specialized facilities (such as cryogenic cooling systems). Research institutions, government agencies, and companies must invest heavily to sustain quantum projects.

o Funding is necessary not only for hardware development but also for quantum software, algorithm research, and workforce training.

2. **Infrastructure and Manufacturing Requirements**:

o Quantum hardware, particularly systems that use superconducting qubits, requires specialized manufacturing facilities and advanced fabrication techniques. Producing high-quality qubits with minimal defects is challenging, and scaling up production adds to the difficulty.

o Quantum labs also require elaborate setups, including shielding from electromagnetic interference, vibration control, and precise temperature regulation, adding to infrastructure costs.

3. **Lack of Skilled Workforce**:

o The demand for professionals skilled in quantum computing is growing rapidly, but educational programs and training opportunities are still limited. Quantum computing requires expertise in physics, mathematics, computer science, and engineering, making it a highly specialized field.

    o Investment in education, training programs, and public-private partnerships is necessary to build a quantum-ready workforce capable of meeting future demands.

4. **Global Competition and Collaboration**:

    o Quantum computing has become a priority in global technological competition, with countries like the United States, China, and European nations investing heavily in quantum initiatives. This competition drives innovation but also creates barriers to open collaboration and knowledge sharing.

    o Effective international collaboration, alongside government support, can accelerate progress while ensuring that quantum technologies are developed responsibly and equitably.

Scalability challenges require a combination of infrastructure, workforce development, and investment in manufacturing and facilities to support quantum computing's transition from lab-scale experiments to industrial-scale systems.

Ongoing Research and Potential Solutions

While these challenges are significant, researchers are actively exploring solutions to overcome them:

1. **Error Correction Advances**:
   - New quantum error-correcting codes, such as **surface codes** and **topological codes**, are being researched to improve error resilience. These codes aim to reduce the number of physical qubits required for error correction, making error correction more feasible for large-scale systems.
   - Researchers are also exploring fault-tolerant architectures that can operate reliably even in the presence of errors, which is essential for scaling quantum computers.

2. **Alternative Qubit Technologies**:
   - While superconducting qubits are currently the most common, other types of qubits—such as **ion-trap qubits**, **photonic qubits**, and **topological qubits**—offer distinct advantages in stability and scalability. Ion-trap qubits, for example, have longer coherence times, while photonic qubits operate at room temperature.
   - Exploring alternative qubit types could lead to more scalable and accessible quantum computing systems, reducing the reliance on cryogenic cooling and specialized infrastructure.

3. **Hybrid Quantum-Classical Systems**:

   o Hybrid systems, which combine quantum and classical computing, can harness the strengths of both types of computing. For instance, **variational quantum algorithms** leverage classical optimizers to reduce the quantum resources required for certain tasks.

   o These hybrid models allow companies to take advantage of quantum computing's capabilities without needing fully fault-tolerant quantum systems, providing practical applications in the near term.

4. **Improved Quantum Software and Development Tools**:

   o Companies like IBM, Google, and Microsoft are actively developing quantum programming languages (e.g., **Qiskit, Cirq**, and **Q#**) and quantum cloud platforms to make quantum computing more accessible. Enhanced programming tools, simulators, and debugging features are reducing the learning curve for quantum developers.

   o Research into software optimization, compilers, and quantum algorithms continues to make quantum programming more practical and efficient, enabling developers to design algorithms that work with existing quantum hardware limitations.

These research initiatives are steadily pushing quantum computing closer to practical applications, with each breakthrough bringing the technology closer to overcoming its current limitations.

Real-World Analogy: Comparing the Current Stage of Quantum Computing to Early Classical Computing

Quantum computing today can be compared to the early days of classical computing, when computers were large, expensive, and limited in functionality:

1. **The Early Mainframe Era**:
   - In the 1940s and 1950s, classical computers like ENIAC and UNIVAC were massive machines that filled entire rooms and required complex cooling systems. They were costly, slow, and specialized, used primarily by governments and research institutions.
   - Similarly, today's quantum computers require large, complex setups with extensive cooling and environmental control. Access to quantum systems is limited to a few labs and institutions due to the high cost and infrastructure requirements.

2. **Limited Applications**:

- o Early classical computers had limited applications, often performing simple calculations or specific tasks for military or scientific purposes. Quantum computing is currently in a similar stage, with most applications focused on highly specialized problems, such as optimization and molecular simulation.

- o Just as classical computing evolved to support general-purpose applications, quantum computing is expected to develop more diverse and practical use cases as technology improves.

3. **The Challenge of Scalability**:

- o In the early days of classical computing, scaling up required innovation in hardware, programming languages, and user interfaces. The shift from mainframes to microcomputers in the 1970s enabled widespread access to computing, driving the digital revolution.

- o Quantum computing faces similar scalability challenges. Overcoming these will require advancements in quantum hardware, error correction, programming languages, and infrastructure, leading to more accessible and practical quantum systems.

4. **The Potential for Transformation**:

- o Just as classical computing transformed industries and revolutionized science, quantum computing has the potential to create a similar impact, particularly in fields like cryptography, drug discovery, and artificial intelligence.

o The journey of quantum computing may be long, but its potential to solve previously intractable problems is driving continued investment, research, and innovation.

This analogy illustrates that quantum computing, while still in its infancy, could eventually become as integral to society as classical computing. The challenges it faces today may seem formidable, but similar barriers were overcome in the evolution of classical computing, underscoring the importance of persistence and innovation.

In this chapter, we explored the major challenges facing **quantum computing**, including technical and physical barriers like qubit stability, error rates, and cooling requirements, as well as practical challenges related to funding, infrastructure, and scalability. We examined how the high cost of development, the need for specialized infrastructure, and the shortage of a skilled workforce are all obstacles to quantum computing's growth.

We also discussed ongoing research and potential solutions, including advances in quantum error correction, alternative qubit technologies, hybrid quantum-classical systems, and improved quantum software. Finally, we drew a comparison between the current stage of quantum computing and the early days of classical computing, illustrating that while quantum technology has a long way to go, its potential impact justifies the challenges and investments.

In the next chapter, we'll look at **the environmental impact of quantum computing**, assessing both its energy requirements and potential environmental benefits as it scales up and becomes more widely used.

CHAPTER 20: THE FUTURE OF QUANTUM COMPUTING

As we conclude this exploration of quantum computing, it's clear that the field is advancing rapidly, with the potential to transform industries and solve complex problems that are currently out of reach for classical computers. The future of quantum computing is filled with both opportunities and challenges. In this final chapter, we'll look at predictions for quantum computing over the next 5–10 years, its role in hybrid computing environments, the potential societal impacts of quantum technology, and resources for those interested in continuing their quantum computing journey.

Predictions for Quantum Computing in the Next 5–10 Years

Quantum computing is evolving at a remarkable pace. While the technology is still in its early stages, several key developments are expected within the next decade:

1. **Increased Qubit Count and Stability**:
   - o Over the next few years, quantum computers will continue to increase in qubit count, with improvements in **qubit stability** and **coherence times**. Companies like IBM, Google, and Rigetti have set ambitious goals to reach qubit counts in the

thousands, which would enable more complex computations.

- ○ By 2030, we may see the development of quantum systems with enough qubits to perform useful computations for specialized applications, even if they are not fully error-corrected.

2. **Enhanced Quantum Error Correction**:

- ○ Researchers will continue working on advanced **quantum error correction** techniques to improve the reliability of quantum systems. As these methods evolve, they will reduce the number of physical qubits needed for error correction, making large-scale quantum computations more practical.

- ○ We may also see the emergence of fault-tolerant quantum systems by the end of the decade, which would allow for more reliable and scalable quantum computing.

3. **Development of Specialized Quantum Applications**:

- ○ Initially, quantum computers will be used for niche applications in areas like **optimization, molecular simulation**, and **machine learning**. By focusing on specific problems that benefit from quantum speedups, companies will start to deploy quantum solutions in real-world scenarios.

- o Industries such as pharmaceuticals, finance, and energy are expected to see early benefits, with applications ranging from drug discovery and portfolio optimization to energy grid management.

4. **Growth of Quantum Cloud Services**:
   - o The next 5–10 years will likely see a rapid expansion of **quantum cloud services**. Companies like IBM, Google, and Amazon already offer quantum computing access via the cloud, allowing organizations to experiment with quantum algorithms without owning quantum hardware.
   - o Quantum cloud services will democratize access to quantum computing, enabling a broader range of users to test and develop quantum applications.

5. **Standardization and Quantum Safe Cryptography**:
   - o As quantum technology advances, there will be a stronger push toward **standardization** in quantum-safe cryptographic algorithms to prepare for potential quantum threats to current encryption.
   - o Governments, industries, and security organizations will continue to work on adopting post-quantum cryptographic standards, ensuring data security in a post-quantum world.

These predictions indicate that while fully scalable, fault-tolerant quantum computing may be further down the line, significant advances in quantum technology will make it increasingly relevant over the next decade.

Quantum Computing's Role in Hybrid Computing Environments

As quantum computing becomes more accessible, it will likely be integrated into **hybrid computing environments** that combine classical, quantum, and possibly even neuromorphic computing:

1. **Quantum-Classical Hybrid Models**:
   - Hybrid quantum-classical systems leverage both quantum and classical computing to tackle complex problems, utilizing quantum computing where it offers an advantage and relying on classical resources for tasks better suited to classical processors.
   - **Variational Quantum Algorithms (VQAs)** are an example of this model, where a classical computer optimizes quantum circuits to solve specific problems, such as finding molecular energy states or optimizing complex systems.

2. **Quantum Accelerators for Specialized Tasks**:

- Just as GPUs serve as accelerators for graphics and deep learning, quantum processors could function as accelerators for specific tasks within a classical computing system.
- In this role, quantum computers may be used as "coprocessors" for classical systems, handling parts of computations that benefit from quantum capabilities, such as simulating quantum systems or solving optimization problems.

3. **Integration with Cloud Computing**:
   - Quantum computing will increasingly integrate with **cloud platforms**, allowing businesses and researchers to access quantum processors through cloud services like Amazon Braket, IBM Quantum, and Google's Quantum AI. This setup provides scalable, on-demand access to quantum resources without requiring users to invest in specialized hardware.

4. **Synergies with Emerging Technologies**:
   - Quantum computing will complement other emerging technologies, such as **artificial intelligence (AI)**, **machine learning (ML)**, and **blockchain**. Quantum-enhanced AI could lead to more powerful models, while quantum computing

might improve blockchain security and transaction speeds.

- o Hybrid environments that combine quantum computing with AI could address complex data analysis and pattern recognition problems that are currently computationally intensive, such as climate modeling, genomics, and predictive analytics.

Hybrid quantum-classical computing environments represent a practical approach to adopting quantum technology in the short term, allowing industries to capitalize on quantum advantages while leveraging existing classical infrastructure.

Potential Societal Impacts of Quantum Technology

The societal impacts of quantum computing could be profound, affecting everything from data security to scientific discovery:

1. **Enhanced Data Security and Privacy**:
   - o Quantum computing's ability to break classical encryption could have significant implications for data security. To address this challenge, post-quantum cryptography will be essential to protect sensitive information in finance, healthcare, government, and other sectors.

- o Quantum cryptography, including **quantum key distribution (QKD)**, could provide theoretically unbreakable encryption, enhancing data privacy and securing communications.

2. **Accelerated Scientific and Medical Discoveries**:

- o Quantum computers could enable breakthroughs in **materials science**, **pharmaceuticals**, and **biotechnology**. For instance, quantum simulations could help discover new materials for energy storage, create more effective drugs, and provide insights into molecular structures and biological processes.

- o These advancements could lead to improved treatments for diseases, more efficient energy solutions, and the development of environmentally friendly materials.

3. **Impact on Workforce and Education**:

- o As quantum computing advances, demand for a quantum-literate workforce will increase. Universities and educational institutions are already beginning to incorporate quantum courses, with an emphasis on interdisciplinary knowledge in physics, computer science, and mathematics.

- o Quantum computing will also create new job roles and career paths, including **quantum software engineers**, **quantum algorithm developers**, and

quantum hardware specialists. Workforce development programs will be essential for preparing a generation of professionals equipped to work with quantum technologies.

4. **Influence on Global Economic and Geopolitical Landscape**:

   o Quantum computing has become a strategic priority for many countries, as it offers potential advantages in **cybersecurity**, **intelligence**, and **economic competitiveness**. Nations investing heavily in quantum technology, such as the United States, China, and members of the European Union, are positioning themselves to lead in quantum innovation.

   o Quantum breakthroughs could redefine global power dynamics, particularly in sectors such as finance, national defense, and scientific research. International collaboration, ethical standards, and equitable access will be important in ensuring that quantum technology benefits society as a whole.

Quantum computing's societal impacts extend far beyond its immediate technical applications, offering both opportunities and challenges that will shape the future of data security, science, the workforce, and global relations.

Final Thoughts and Resources for Continued Learning in Quantum Computing

Quantum computing is a complex and rapidly evolving field, and staying informed requires ongoing learning. Here are some final thoughts and resources for those interested in deepening their knowledge:

1. **The Importance of Patience and Persistence**:
    - Quantum computing is in its early stages, much like classical computing was decades ago. Progress is often incremental, requiring patience and sustained research. However, each breakthrough brings quantum technology closer to practical applications, making it an exciting time to learn about and contribute to the field.
2. **Recommended Learning Resources**:
    - **Books**:
        - *Quantum Computation and Quantum Information* by Michael Nielsen and Isaac Chuang – A foundational text in quantum computing.
        - *Quantum Computing for Computer Scientists* by Noson S. Yanofsky and Mirco

A. Mannucci – An accessible introduction to the theory behind quantum computing.

- **Online Courses**:
  - **Qiskit Global Summer School** (IBM): A two-week intensive course on quantum computing fundamentals and quantum programming.
  - **MITx - Quantum Information Science I & II**: Offers an in-depth exploration of quantum computing and quantum information science.
  - **Quantum Computing and Quantum Information (Coursera)** by the University of Toronto: An introductory course covering the basics of quantum computing.
- **Tutorials and Platforms**:
  - **IBM Quantum Experience**: A free platform with access to IBM's quantum computers, allowing users to run experiments and learn quantum programming with Qiskit.
  - **Microsoft's Quantum Development Kit and Q#**: Offers resources, tutorials, and tools for programming quantum applications.
  - **Google's Cirq**: A framework for building quantum circuits, with resources and documentation to help users get started.

3. **Staying Updated**:

   o Quantum computing is an active area of research, with new developments and breakthroughs occurring regularly. Following scientific journals, industry blogs, and quantum-focused publications can help enthusiasts stay informed about the latest advancements.

   o Attending conferences, webinars, and workshops is also a valuable way to connect with experts in the field and learn about recent research.

4. **Engaging with the Quantum Community**:

   o Online forums, communities, and study groups dedicated to quantum computing provide opportunities to ask questions, share knowledge, and collaborate on projects. Platforms like GitHub, Stack Overflow, and Qiskit Community are excellent places to start.

Quantum computing holds the potential to transform numerous fields, and by staying curious and engaged, anyone interested can participate in its development.

In this final chapter, we explored the future of quantum computing, including predictions for the next 5–10 years, the role of quantum computing in hybrid environments, and the potential societal impacts of quantum technology. We discussed how industries and governments are preparing for quantum advancements, how hybrid quantum-classical models will enable practical applications, and the potential effects on data security, scientific discovery, and global power dynamics.

Finally, we provided resources for continued learning, emphasizing the importance of persistence, patience, and community engagement for those interested in pursuing knowledge or careers in quantum computing.

The journey of quantum computing is just beginning, with each new discovery opening doors to possibilities that were once the realm of science fiction. As technology advances, quantum computing will continue to evolve, offering tools to address some of the world's most complex challenges and transforming our understanding of computation itself.

CHAPTER 21: ETHICAL AND PHILOSOPHICAL IMPLICATIONS OF QUANTUM COMPUTING

As quantum computing advances and begins to intersect with fields like artificial intelligence, cybersecurity, and biotechnology, it brings forth a new range of ethical, philosophical, and societal questions. Beyond the technical challenges and practical applications, quantum computing prompts us to consider how this transformative technology will impact society, how it should be governed, and how we can ensure it is developed responsibly. In this final, reflective chapter, we'll explore the ethical and philosophical implications of quantum computing, the responsibility of scientists and developers, and frameworks for guiding its ethical development.

The Nature of Knowledge and Reality in Quantum Computing

Quantum computing, rooted in the principles of **quantum mechanics**, challenges our classical understanding of reality. Concepts like **superposition** and **entanglement** defy intuitive logic, raising fundamental questions about the nature of knowledge and existence.

1. **Quantum Mechanics and the Limits of Human Understanding**:

    o Quantum phenomena don't conform to classical expectations; particles can exist in multiple states simultaneously, and measuring them can affect their behavior. This challenges traditional notions of cause and effect, as well as the idea of objective reality.

    o Philosophers and scientists alike are forced to confront questions about the limits of human perception and whether we can ever truly understand the quantum world.

2. **Computational Complexity and Consciousness**:

    o Some researchers speculate that quantum computing could one day offer insights into complex systems like the human brain. Could quantum principles play a role in consciousness or cognition? While this idea remains speculative, the philosophical implications of a "quantum mind" are profound and raise questions about the intersection between human intelligence and machine intelligence.

    o If quantum computers can model or replicate cognitive processes, this could shift our understanding of consciousness and challenge what it means to be "intelligent" or "aware."

3. **Reality Simulation Hypothesis**:

○ Quantum computing's ability to simulate complex systems has led some to wonder whether the universe itself operates like a quantum computer or is, in fact, a vast simulation. This hypothesis, while highly speculative, invites philosophical debate about the nature of existence and reality.

○ If quantum computing allows us to simulate systems down to atomic or even subatomic levels, could we one day simulate realities as complex as our own? The ethical implications of simulated consciousness, reality, and existence could challenge human assumptions about life and identity.

Ethical Considerations in the Development of Quantum Technology

As quantum computing holds the potential to disrupt fields like cybersecurity, healthcare, and AI, ethical considerations must play a central role in its development:

1. **Data Privacy and Security**:
   ○ The ability of quantum computers to break classical encryption could expose private data, posing a significant ethical challenge. If not managed responsibly, the power to decrypt sensitive data

could be misused, compromising personal privacy and organizational security.

- o Ethical frameworks are needed to balance quantum technology's potential benefits with the need to protect individuals' and organizations' rights to data privacy.

2. **Algorithmic Bias and Fairness**:

- o Quantum algorithms, like their classical counterparts, can inadvertently incorporate biases. As quantum machine learning and AI evolve, ethical guidelines must be in place to ensure fair and unbiased outcomes, particularly in applications like healthcare, hiring, and criminal justice.

- o Developers and researchers have a responsibility to ensure that quantum algorithms don't reinforce existing biases or create new ones, and that they are transparent, explainable, and fair.

3. **Environmental Impact and Sustainability**:

- o Quantum computing infrastructure, particularly systems requiring extreme cooling, can be resource-intensive. As quantum technology scales, its environmental impact will become a more significant consideration.

- o Ethical and sustainable practices in the development and operation of quantum technology will be important to mitigate energy consumption, reduce carbon emissions, and promote long-term sustainability.

4. **Equity and Access**:

   o Quantum computing could widen the digital divide, with access limited to wealthy nations, corporations, and institutions. Ensuring that quantum technology benefits society equitably is an ethical imperative.

   o Policies, regulations, and global cooperation can help democratize access to quantum technology, preventing monopolization and ensuring it serves a diverse range of needs and communities.

Guidelines and Governance for Ethical Quantum Computing

Developing ethical frameworks and governance models for quantum computing is crucial to address its potential risks and ensure responsible development:

1. **Global Collaboration and Governance**:

   o Quantum technology's potential impact on security, economics, and science makes international cooperation essential. Establishing global standards for quantum research, development, and deployment can prevent misuse and promote equitable access.

- The creation of organizations similar to the **International Atomic Energy Agency (IAEA)** for quantum technology could be valuable in fostering transparency, collaboration, and shared ethical standards.

2. **Ethics Boards and Review Panels**:
   - Establishing ethics review panels specifically for quantum computing could help ensure that research and applications align with societal values and ethical principles.
   - These boards could offer guidance on quantum research projects, assess potential impacts on privacy and security, and advise on the ethical implications of quantum applications in AI, cryptography, and healthcare.

3. **Incorporating Ethical Education in Quantum Training**:
   - Integrating ethical education into quantum computing programs could prepare future researchers and developers to think critically about the ethical and societal impacts of their work.
   - Universities, institutions, and quantum education platforms should include modules on the ethical considerations of quantum technology, emphasizing responsible innovation and societal impact.

Societal Impact and Public Awareness of Quantum Technology

As quantum computing evolves, its societal impact will likely grow, creating a need for public awareness and engagement:

1. **Public Understanding and Education**:
   - Quantum computing concepts can be challenging for the public to understand, which may limit the ability to engage in discussions about its societal impact. Efforts to make quantum concepts accessible and relevant to everyday concerns will be crucial.
   - Educational programs, public forums, and accessible media can help demystify quantum computing, enabling more people to participate in discussions about its ethical and societal implications.

2. **Job Creation and Workforce Development**:
   - Quantum computing will create new job roles and require specialized skills, impacting the workforce across various sectors. Ensuring that workers have access to quantum education and training can help them adapt to these changes.
   - Policymakers and educational institutions should collaborate to develop programs that support workforce development and provide resources for individuals transitioning into quantum-related fields.

3. **Impacts on Inequality and Global Disparity**:

   o Quantum technology's impact on fields like finance, healthcare, and national defense could exacerbate global disparities if access is limited to wealthy nations and organizations.

   o Policies that prioritize equitable access to quantum resources and ensure that quantum technology benefits diverse communities can help prevent these inequalities and promote global stability.

Final Thoughts: Quantum Computing as a Transformative Force
Quantum computing has the potential to be one of the most transformative technologies in human history, reshaping industries, scientific understanding, and daily life. While the road to fully realized quantum technology is complex and filled with challenges, the progress made thus far hints at a future where quantum computing could solve problems that were previously unsolvable, drive scientific discovery, and catalyze innovation across domains.

At this pivotal stage, scientists, policymakers, educators, and the public have a shared responsibility to ensure that quantum computing is developed ethically, sustainably, and inclusively. Quantum technology presents a powerful opportunity, but with that power comes the responsibility to safeguard its development for the common good. By considering the ethical, philosophical, and societal impacts of quantum computing, we can work toward a future where quantum technology benefits humanity as a whole.

In this reflective final chapter, we explored the ethical and philosophical implications of **quantum computing** and its potential impact on society. We discussed how quantum computing challenges traditional understandings of reality, knowledge, and consciousness and examined its ethical considerations, including data privacy, environmental impact, fairness, and equitable access.

We highlighted the importance of establishing ethical frameworks, global governance, and public awareness to guide quantum computing's development responsibly. With ethical education, collaborative governance, and public engagement, quantum technology can be directed toward equitable and beneficial uses, avoiding the pitfalls of past technological revolutions.

As quantum computing advances, its impact will be far-reaching, shaping the future of science, technology, and society. By approaching its development with ethical foresight and a commitment to societal benefit, we can ensure that quantum computing becomes a transformative force for good, enhancing human understanding and driving progress in ways that align with our collective values.

CHAPTER 22: QUANTUM COMPUTING AND ARTIFICIAL INTELLIGENCE

The convergence of **quantum computing** and **artificial intelligence (AI)** represents a new frontier in technological advancement. By leveraging the unique capabilities of quantum systems, quantum computing could revolutionize how we approach AI, especially in areas that require vast amounts of data processing and complex optimization. In this chapter, we'll delve into how quantum computing could transform AI, explore quantum machine learning (QML) algorithms, examine real-world applications of quantum-enhanced AI, and discuss the challenges and ethical implications of combining these two transformative technologies.

How Quantum Computing Could Transform AI

Quantum computing holds promise for enhancing AI by tackling computational bottlenecks that limit current AI capabilities:

1. **Accelerated Data Processing**:
   - Quantum computers can process data in parallel through **quantum superposition**, enabling them to perform certain tasks exponentially faster than

classical computers. This ability could allow quantum computers to analyze large datasets more quickly, improving the efficiency of AI training and analysis.

o By accelerating matrix operations and other computationally intensive tasks in AI, quantum computers could significantly reduce the time needed to train machine learning models.

2. **Improved Optimization**:

o Many AI applications, particularly in machine learning, involve solving optimization problems, such as adjusting model parameters for the best fit. Quantum computing can address optimization tasks more efficiently with algorithms like **Grover's search algorithm** and **quantum annealing**, which allow faster convergence on optimal solutions.

o Quantum optimization could help fine-tune large-scale neural networks and find more effective solutions to problems that would be computationally intensive for classical systems.

3. **Quantum Machine Learning (QML)**:

o Quantum computing enables new approaches to machine learning, including **quantum-enhanced neural networks**, **quantum support vector machines (QSVMs)**, and **quantum principal**

component analysis (QPCA). These quantum algorithms can handle high-dimensional data more efficiently, potentially improving accuracy and speed for applications in areas like image recognition, natural language processing, and recommendation systems.

- o QML could redefine how machine learning models are developed and applied, especially in fields where data complexity and scale pose significant challenges.

4. **Simulating Complex Systems**:
- o Quantum computers are particularly well-suited for simulating complex quantum systems, which could benefit AI applications in fields like **drug discovery**, **materials science**, and **climate modeling**. By simulating quantum interactions, quantum-enhanced AI could provide insights into these systems more accurately than classical computers.

Quantum Machine Learning Algorithms and Their Applications

Quantum machine learning is a promising area within AI that leverages quantum algorithms to improve efficiency, scalability, and accuracy. Here are some key quantum machine learning algorithms and their potential applications:

1. **Quantum Neural Networks (QNNs)**:
   - ○ Quantum neural networks are similar to classical neural networks but use qubits and quantum gates to represent neurons and weights. QNNs are particularly promising for tasks that involve large data sets and complex patterns, as quantum superposition and entanglement can enhance data processing capabilities.
   - ○ **Applications**: Image and pattern recognition, predictive modeling, and natural language processing.

2. **Quantum Support Vector Machines (QSVMs)**:
   - ○ QSVMs extend classical support vector machines by leveraging quantum kernels that project data into high-dimensional quantum states, making it easier to separate data classes. This approach can handle complex data structures that would be challenging for classical SVMs.
   - ○ **Applications**: Fraud detection, medical diagnosis, and classification tasks in high-dimensional data sets.

3. **Quantum Principal Component Analysis (QPCA)**:
   - ○ QPCA is a quantum adaptation of classical principal component analysis (PCA), which is used for dimensionality reduction. QPCA can process large datasets more efficiently by finding the principal

components of data in a high-dimensional quantum state.

- o **Applications**: Feature extraction, data compression, and noise reduction in large datasets, such as genomic or financial data.

4. **Variational Quantum Classifier (VQC)**:

- o The VQC is a hybrid quantum-classical model that uses quantum circuits to classify data. The variational circuit optimizes parameters to minimize classification error, making it suitable for supervised learning tasks.

- o **Applications**: Image classification, sentiment analysis, and financial forecasting.

By incorporating these quantum algorithms, quantum machine learning has the potential to solve problems that are currently intractable or resource-intensive for classical systems.

Real-World Applications of Quantum-Enhanced AI

The integration of quantum computing with AI is still in its experimental phase, but early applications show promise in several key fields:

1. **Healthcare and Drug Discovery**:

- o Quantum-enhanced AI could transform drug discovery by simulating molecular structures and identifying promising compounds. AI algorithms, powered by quantum computing, can analyze molecular interactions more accurately, reducing the need for trial and error in drug development.
- o Companies like Pfizer and Roche are exploring how quantum AI can accelerate the discovery of new medications, potentially reducing costs and improving patient outcomes.

2. **Finance and Risk Analysis**:
   - o Financial institutions are experimenting with quantum-enhanced AI to improve risk analysis, fraud detection, and portfolio optimization. Quantum machine learning can process vast amounts of financial data to detect patterns, predict market trends, and optimize investments.
   - o JPMorgan Chase, for example, is investing in quantum AI to analyze large-scale market data and improve decision-making accuracy in financial modeling.

3. **Climate Modeling and Environmental Science**:
   - o Quantum AI has the potential to model complex environmental systems with greater precision. By combining AI with quantum simulations, researchers

could create more accurate climate models, leading to better predictions and insights into climate change.

- o Applications include modeling atmospheric conditions, forecasting weather patterns, and analyzing ecological changes to inform conservation efforts.

4. **Cybersecurity and Threat Detection**:
   - o Quantum-enhanced AI could bolster cybersecurity by analyzing network data to detect anomalies and identify potential threats faster than classical systems. Quantum algorithms can accelerate threat detection and response, protecting against cyberattacks in real time.
   - o Companies like IBM are investigating how quantum-enhanced AI could improve the speed and accuracy of threat detection systems.

These applications illustrate the transformative potential of quantum-enhanced AI across a wide range of industries, from healthcare to finance to environmental science.

Challenges and Ethical Considerations in Quantum AI

The combination of quantum computing and AI brings both technical and ethical challenges:

1. **Technical Challenges**:
   - o Quantum hardware is still in development, and current quantum computers have limited qubit counts and high error rates. These limitations make it difficult to apply quantum AI at scale, especially for complex tasks that require reliable, large-scale quantum systems.
   - o Quantum algorithms are highly specialized, requiring expertise in both quantum mechanics and AI. As quantum AI research progresses, there will be a growing need for hybrid skills that combine these two domains.

2. **Data Privacy and Security**:
   - o Quantum AI applications, particularly in finance and healthcare, involve sensitive data. With quantum computers' potential to break traditional encryption, protecting data privacy in quantum AI applications is essential.
   - o Researchers and organizations will need to implement **quantum-safe cryptographic methods** to protect data in quantum-AI-enabled systems, ensuring privacy and security for users.

3. **Algorithmic Bias and Fairness**:
   - o AI algorithms, including quantum-enhanced ones, can inadvertently introduce biases, particularly in

applications like healthcare, hiring, and criminal justice. Quantum AI systems must be designed with fairness and transparency in mind to prevent these biases from affecting outcomes.

o Ethical oversight and guidelines are necessary to ensure that quantum AI applications are developed responsibly, with considerations for fairness and social impact.

4. **Resource and Accessibility Inequities**:

o Quantum AI development requires substantial resources, making it accessible only to well-funded organizations and nations. This exclusivity could widen the digital divide, particularly if quantum AI applications benefit only a select few.

o Ensuring equitable access to quantum AI resources and addressing potential socioeconomic impacts will be important for the ethical development of this technology.

These challenges highlight the need for interdisciplinary collaboration and ethical frameworks to guide the responsible development of quantum AI.

The Future of Quantum-Enhanced AI

Quantum-enhanced AI is an emerging field that holds significant promise for the future of artificial intelligence. Here are some possible directions for quantum AI in the coming years:

1. **Specialized Quantum AI Applications**:
   - Quantum AI will likely focus on niche applications that benefit from quantum speedups, such as materials discovery, personalized medicine, and financial forecasting. As quantum technology matures, these applications will become more prevalent across industries.

2. **Development of Hybrid AI Models**:
   - The future of quantum AI will likely involve hybrid models that combine quantum and classical AI algorithms, leveraging quantum computing where it offers a distinct advantage. Hybrid models provide a more practical approach to integrating quantum AI in the near term.

3. **Cross-Disciplinary Research in Quantum and AI**:
   - The convergence of quantum computing and AI will require collaboration across physics, computer science, mathematics, and ethics. Universities and research institutions are already beginning to establish interdisciplinary programs that prepare students and researchers for work in quantum AI.

4. **Ethical Standards and Governance for Quantum AI**:

  o As quantum AI develops, there will be an increasing need for ethical standards, transparency, and governance to guide its application in society. Organizations like the IEEE and the Partnership on AI are well-positioned to provide guidance for responsible quantum AI development.

The future of quantum-enhanced AI will depend on advancements in both quantum hardware and AI algorithms, as well as thoughtful ethical considerations to ensure that the technology is used responsibly and equitably.

In this chapter, we explored the intersection of **quantum computing** and **artificial intelligence**, examining how quantum technology could transform AI by accelerating data processing, enhancing optimization, and enabling new approaches in machine learning. We discussed key quantum machine learning algorithms, such as quantum neural networks and quantum support vector machines, and examined their applications in fields like healthcare, finance, climate modeling, and cybersecurity.

We also considered the challenges and ethical implications of combining quantum computing with AI, from data privacy and algorithmic fairness to the resource inequities that may arise in a quantum-powered future. Finally, we looked at the future of quantum-enhanced AI, which will likely involve hybrid quantum-classical systems, specialized applications, and the establishment of ethical standards to guide responsible development.

The fusion of quantum computing and AI promises to be one of the most transformative developments in technology, reshaping industries and providing tools to address some of society's most complex challenges. With careful, ethical stewardship, quantum-enhanced AI could open new doors in science, medicine, and beyond, leading us into a new era of intelligent, quantum-powered innovation.